YOU CAN
CHANGE
THE WORLD

YOU CAN

CHANGE

THE WORLD

Keys to Stepping
Into Your Destiny

Claudia Wintoch

DESTINY IMAGE™ EUROPE srl
Via Maiella, 1
66020 San Giovanni Teatino (Ch) – Italy

"Changing the world, one book at a time."

This book and all other Destiny Image™ Europe books are available at Christian bookstores and distributors worldwide.

To order products, or for any other correspondence:

DESTINY IMAGE™ EUROPE srl
Via della Scafa 29/14
65013 Città Sant'Angelo (Pe) Italy
Tel. +39 085 4716623 • +39 085 8670146
Email: info@eurodestinyimage.com
Or reach us on the Internet: www.eurodestinyimage.com

ISBN: 978-88-96727-22-5
For Worldwide Distribution, Printed in the U.S.A.
1 2 3 4 5 6 / 14 13 12 11

Dedication

Dedicated to Jill Austin, my beloved mentor and spiritual mom, who got a glimpse of her Beloved and decided to stay with Him forever.

Contents

Foreword

The first two letters of the English words "good" and "God" are GO. "Go" is the first word in the Great Commission. Going is the activity of faith, motivated by love.

God's first words to the first believer were, "Go forth!" Abraham, the father of all who believe, went even though he didn't know where he was going. Faith involves a journey. It starts with leaving—going and seeing. It culminates in becoming a force of blessing.

The first two Hebrew words in Genesis 12:1 are *lech lecha*, which may be translated, "Go yourself." The implication is that there is something about leaving the familiar, the comfortable, that allows us to find ourselves, our purpose.

Stuck in the middle of all that was familiar in ancient Mesopotamia, Abram was just another member of his family and culture, bound by the norms of everyday life. However, God invaded his predictable world with the words, *Go forth!* The Amplified Bible captures the implications in its rendering of Genesis 12:1:

> ...*Go for yourself* [for your own advantage] *away from your country, from your relatives and your father's house, to the land that I will show you.*

It is to our advantage to leave the familiar and follow the Divine Whisper. He speaks to the heart of every true seeker who knows deep inside that there is a more glorious reality waiting to be released. Through the simple and sometimes heroic activities that spring from love and faith, God's Kingdom comes.

In the going, we find ourselves. The unfamiliar journey of faith is the soil in which each of our destinies sprouts, grows, and bears the fruit that changes the world. The "going" has purpose. We go forth from all that is familiar. We go forth to the land of vision, the place that God allows us to see. In the land of vision, He makes something of us. His creative capacity is released in our going. He makes us something great, and His divine favor and blessing takes hold of us and is put into full affect. In our going, He makes each of us into an agent of restitution, justice, and the re-creation of the world—until the whole earth is filled with His glory. He makes us the blessing. From within us, through our seemingly insignificant nobody lives, it is possible that all the families of the earth will experience the blessing of the One who made them!

Claudia Wintoch heard the whisper. She went where no one wanted to go.

Most people have dreams and desires to make the world a better place. Yet, very few translate their dreams into a clear vision, and fewer still put their vision into action. The obstacles and objections are so great, the path is not always clear. Because of various difficulties, God-given dreams languish until the nudges and urgings wither and finally cease.

But what if? What happens when a person casts aside all the reasons why not and unreasonably pursues the possibilities? This is faith. This is love translated into action. Despite the odds and the Goliaths standing in the way, one small, insignificant David changed the course of a nation and all of history. That's always been the way God works.

But God has chosen the foolish things of the world to put to shame the wise, and God has chosen the weak things of the world to put to shame the things which are mighty; and the base things of the world and the things which are despised God has chosen, and the things which are not, to bring to nothing the things that are, that no flesh should glory in His presence (1 Corinthians 1:27-29 NKJV).

In this book unfolds the heartfelt journey of a neglected, abused, and overlooked young woman who became possessed by the love of God and wouldn't stop until she turned desires into history. In some sense, this is the story of every believer who carries the dreams of God within their hearts.

Today, Claudia Wintoch has been working in Mali, a country in West Africa, for almost a decade. She went as a single woman into one of the poorest nations on earth—where less than 1 percent of the population is Christian, where child sacrifice is still commonly practiced, and where she knew not one person! In a few years, she developed a beautiful haven for children, especially young boys, who are rescued from the streets of Bamako, the capital of Mali. God's grace has changed their world. These children are the future of a nation, young Daniels and Esthers! They are being educated and discipled in an outpost of Heaven, where the tangible presence of God is a daily reality.

This is Claudia's story, which began in Vienna, Austria, in abuse and despair, progressing into the university years of a lost and lonely girl. Darkness gave way to light in transforming encounters with Jesus. When He comes, everything changes. She became a lover of God and a pilgrim on a journey into His will for her life.

As you read *You Can Change the World*, you will find keys for identifying and unlocking your own destiny. Claudia takes you through the process of her own preparation for total immersion into God's plan for her life, the healing of the heart, and the prophetic encounters that totally wrecked her for anything less than the beauty of God.

In her story, you will find the eternal pattern. And your story may change forever!

Charles Stock
Author, *Glow in the Dark*
Senior Pastor, *Life Center*
Harrisburg, Pennsylvania

Chapter One

Why Change the World?

Why Change the World?

When we turn on our televisions to watch the news, we are bombarded with information about natural disasters, crimes, and tragedies around the world. When we open our newspapers, we find the same. When we see homeless people, prostitutes, people who are suffering, it certainly looks like our world is in a bad shape.

But God created this world beautiful, a paradise meant for our enjoyment; the perfect environment for a perfect relationship between the Creator and the created. Can you imagine His excitement and anticipation as He created another part of the earth every day, making it more and more beautiful, the perfect setting for his masterpiece. Every day He looked at His work and said that it was good (see Gen. 1).

Then finally, the big day had come. Everything was prepared—the waters, the land, the plants, and the animals. Only one thing was missing— the one creature He had made everything for; the one creature He had had in mind from the first day as He hovered over the formless planet to make something beautiful out of it; the one creature He longed to have fellowship with and created for this specific purpose—humankind. God gave of Himself as He created man and woman in His own image.

This was not just another creature designed by ingenious creativity of our amazing God. No, this creature resembled the all-powerful Creator of the universe, the One who has no beginning and no end, the One who is beyond time, the One we cannot even fathom. God put everything into this creature who was created by love and for love. And then He breathed into him, giving him a spirit, a part of Himself that no other creature could claim.

Oh what a wondrous day! What a glorious moment as man came to life! He opened his eyes and looked into the eyes of his Maker. What did he see? Did he see tears of joy and pride as the Trinity looked upon their new object of affection? If you've ever seen a father looking at his newborn child, you've seen a glimpse of what God must have looked like that day. But Adam was no child; he was an adult, and the first glimpse of life he was given was the beautiful eyes of love of his Creator. He was perfect, he was loved, he was secure, he was safe, the whole pride of his Father. He was in perfect relationship and union with the One who was all-sufficient and in need of nothing, yet with the greatest desire of unbroken relationship with the one He created in His image.

Then and Now

Now you may be thinking, *Nice story, but it has nothing whatever to do with my reality. What happened? Why is this not what our world looks like today? Why are the tears in God's eyes today not tears of love and pride, but instead tears of a Father's broken heart?*

For Adam's love for His Creator to be meaningful at all, it had to be by his choice. For example, imagine that I tell you to walk down a certain road in front of you to its very end and you are to never take any other road. You start walking, passing by houses and trees, until you get to the end of the dead-end street. You never saw any other roads, so you had no choice than to keep going.

Did you obey me? Did you even have a choice but to obey me? No, you didn't. But what if you started walking down this particular road, and then you notice a road to the left that looks very nice, and then you see one to the right that looks even nicer. But you remember my words and keep going straight until you reach the end of the road. Did you obey me? Yes, you did. You had a choice to disobey, but didn't. Your obedience is meaningful in this case.

For Adam's love to be meaningful, he had to be given the choice not to love God, not to obey God, and so he was told he could not eat of just one single tree of the many trees in the Garden, the tree of knowledge of good and evil. Adam lacked nothing at all; he had everything anyone could ever want. He walked with God in the Garden every day. Can you imagine their conversations? A proud Father walking with His son, spending quality time together. However, while everything was perfect, there was an enemy out there waiting for his chance to mess up this beautiful creation of God who he hated so much.

The Enemy

And so the enemy approached Eve, the woman God had created using Adam's rib, twisting God's words and tempting her to eat of the one forbidden tree. Why did she do it? Why did Adam take the fruit from Eve's hand instead of rebuking her? One day in Heaven we'll be able to ask them, I hope. This one moment of disobedience, of choosing to disregard their Creator's love for them by going against His will, of putting themselves and their wills above God's, this one moment when that fateful bite in their mouths was chewed and moved to their stomachs had consequences of cosmic reach, changing the course of history forever.

Their spirits died, their trusting and loving relationship with God was cut off, and God's heart was broken over the loss of His most precious, loved, and cherished children. His children had moved their obedience and allegiance from their wonderful, heavenly Father to the enemy of God who was just a created being wanting to take God's place. The enemy became the "prince of this world" (see John 12:31, 14:30, 16:11), the ruler of the earth, and the king people bowed down to and worshiped. Adam had been chosen to be the prince and ruler of the earth, but he passed on his position to the enemy whose only purpose was and is to hurt God, the Creator of the universe, and what He loves most—His masterpiece creation, humankind.

Death, sickness, and tragedy entered the world as it came under the curse of God and its new ruler. Adam and Eve were banned from the Garden, which was sealed, and hardship became the norm of life. From now on, it would take hard work to eat, and children would be born in pain. From now on, people and animals would die, children would get sick, and natural catastrophes would happen as creation was "in bondage to decay" (Rom. 8:21). Since that day "the whole creation has been groaning as in the pains of childbirth right up to the present time" (Rom. 8:22). Since that day, people choose again and again to serve God's enemy rather than their heavenly Father, resulting in unimaginable pain and suffering and tragedy. Every day in the news we see the results of that fateful day and the choices humankind has made since that day.

Responding in Love

The question is, how do we respond when we see injustice and suffering? It's so very easy and comfortable to simply choose not to look, not to listen, and to hole up in our own little worlds, shutting out world events. After all, what do they have to do with me? These aren't my problems; I have enough worries of my own. Let others deal with them. Let politicians deal with them. Let the Christians "over there" deal with them. Let the intercessors battle the problems out in prayer. It's not my battle.

We have our own little worlds we live in and keep busy there. But what is God's heart? Didn't He say He so loved the *world* that He gave His only Son? Isn't His heart breaking with every tragedy where His children, His masterpiece creation, are being hurt or killed?

Have you ever prayed to have God's heart? If so, then you cannot turn away. You'll be compelled to open your heart to His pain. You'll be compelled to cry out to your heavenly Father for the sake of these people. I remember the times when watching the news would always turn into a prayer meeting for me, as I allowed God to give me His heart. I would lie on the floor in my living room, weeping and interceding for hurting people on the other side of the world, crying out for God's intervention. I also used the newspaper to pray for the world. I'd read an article and then go straight into intercession for that country and the situation described.

What was I doing? I was responding to God's heart. I was changing the world on my knees and my face. Right there in the middle of Vienna, Austria, this little 20-something unimpressive girl with many issues was changing the world. Did anyone see? No. Did anyone know? No. Did it produce accolades and praise from people? No. Did it make a difference? Most definitely.

There will be a lot of surprises once we get to Heaven. People's statuses will be different from the ones they had on earth, and we will meet many great heroes in the faith whose names we never heard this side of Heaven. We will also be surprised at which one of our works will remain and which ones will burn up. God's standards are very different from the world's standards, which we can see throughout His book, His love letter, revealing Himself to us in word, the Bible. We give to get, we die to live, and we go low to be elevated. God loves what we do in secret, only for His eyes to see. Jesus said that those who get their reward from people won't get it from God (see Matt. 6:1). Let's allow Him to break our hearts for what breaks His heart. Yes, it's painful, but it's so worth it!

Once you're sharing God's suffering heart in intercession, you'll feel the pull to actually do something about the need in front of you, whether you can actually do something practical or not. For years I prayed Isaiah's prayer from Isaiah 6 from the depths of my heart. "Here I am, send me!" (Isa. 6:8b). But all I could do at the time was send my money to relieve pain, while my heart longed to go out there and be God's hands, feet, ears, eyes, and mouth to the hurting.

As a young believer, my spirit ears heard the cry of the Lord that has been ringing through the universe for thousands of years. "Whom shall I send? And who will go for us?" Can you hear the pain in His voice? Can you feel His longing? It is a mystery how the all-powerful God has limited Himself to work through His children rather than simply sending a host of angels to take care of the things that cause Him pain.

Is There Anyone?

He wants to partner with us, and so His eyes are looking all over globe (see 2 Chron. 16:9) to find those will listen to His heart's cry and respond. His voice is full of longing, desire, and urgency: "Is there any-one out there who cares as I do? Is there anyone out there who is will-ing to lay down his life and go in My name? Anyone who cares about Me and My purposes more than himself and his own life?"

Sound travels in waveform, and the waves just continue on and on, going from planet to planet and galaxy to galaxy, never disappearing in our infinite universe. The sound of His voice is still filling the universe. Today the Lord is handing out nations to His children. He's telling us, "Ask Me, and I will make the nations your inheritance, the ends of the earth your possession" (Ps. 2:8). Will you answer His heart's cry with the humble request to be given a nation as inheritance? Will you respond to His cry with a resounding YES, even though you know you have noth-ing to offer but yourself?

I did, praying Isaiah's prayer over and over and over again. Lord, send me! Lord, send me where no one wants to go. Send me where every-body else has said no. Send me to the farthest and toughest place where You can't find anyone else who will go. I cannot stand the pain in Your voice any more. I want to fulfill Your heart's desire and go out into the highways and byways to bring in Your Bride, the Bride who has been neglected and forgotten. I want to populate Heaven with Your beloved sons and daughters. I want to see Your glory cover the earth as the waters cover the sea (see Hab. 2:14). I want to see Your Kingdom come on earth as it is Your Heaven, Your will be done on earth (see Matt. 6:10). I want to see Your honor restored among the nations of the world. I want Jesus to be revered, worshiped, and recognized as the King of kings and Lord of lords. I want to see people from every tribe and language and people and nation (see Rev. 5:9) stand around the throne and worship You non-stop. You are holy, You are worthy, You are the Lamb upon the throne!

Will You?

Will you ask Him for the nations? Will you listen to His heart's cry? Will you say, here I am, send me? Do not look upon who you are. Do not look at what you have or don't have. Do not look at your problems, whether financial, emotional, or physical. Isn't He the all powerful God? Can He not change your situation, whatever it is? All He is looking for is somebody who will say yes. Somebody who cares more about Him than himself or herself. Somebody who is ready to lay down his or her life to accomplish His purposes.

The day you say yes to Him, He will start the process of preparation in your life. It may take months, or years, or even decades. There will be times of discouragement and times when you feel like the process has stopped. Times when you will be tempted to change direction or get out of the fire of preparation. There will be times when you feel as if God has forgotten you. There will be times when you feel like the cost is too high. You will be tempted to give up and return to a comfortable lifestyle of not making a difference, only to find out that you have burned your bridges and have nowhere to return to.

Your patience, perseverance, and conviction of your calling will be tested to the breaking point as you labor on toward the vision He has given you—the dream you have hidden in your heart and that seems so far away. But when those times come, you need to fix your eyes on your beautiful Savior, your best Friend, the Lover of your soul, your Bride-groom King, Jesus (see Heb. 12:2), and continue walking toward your destiny, toward the fulfillment of His great calling on your life.

Will it be easy? No. Will it be painless? No. Will it be cheap? No. Will it be worth it? A resounding yes. He is going to take you, the broken clay vessel that you are—whether you are totally broken or only have a few cracks—and put you on the potter's wheel where He will lovingly restore you. He will break off the pieces that need to go, and add others. He will mend the cracks and add color until you resemble the image of His Son, Jesus, until you are the vessel He needs to accomplish His purposes. No vessel is too broken, no vessel beyond repair.

Maybe you have been abused physically, emotionally, or sexually. Maybe you grew up without love. Maybe you did not have a mom or dad. Maybe you never knew God until you were an adult. Maybe you can barely function in daily life. May I tell you secret? All this was true for me. But our heavenly Father picked up this thrown away, discarded little clay pot in the middle of Austria, and all He could see was the beautiful end-product of a vessel resembling His Son. A vessel that could be filled with the greatest treasure (see 2 Cor. 4:7)—His Spirit,

His anointing, His living water—to be poured out into the nations of this earth to advance His Kingdom and prepare His Bride for the glorious return of His Son, the wonderful Bridegroom.

He asks, "Will you go for Me, My son, My daughter?" Say yes today, and start the preparation process to become a world changer without any more delay.

~

Father, I would like to become a world changer and carry Your Kingdom wherever You send me. I offer myself up to You today to do a deep work of preparation within me so I can step into my destiny and fulfill my calling. Thank You for loving me so much that You want to transform me from glory to glory into the reflection of Your Son Jesus.

Change Points

1. God created a paradise meant for your enjoyment; the perfect environment for a perfect relationship between the Creator and the created.

2. God's greatest desire was and is an unbroken relationship with the one He created in His image—you.

3. Death, sickness, and tragedy entered the world as it came under the curse of God and its new ruler.

4. Will you respond to His cry with a resounding YES, even though you know you have nothing to offer but yourself?

5. Your patience, perseverance, and conviction of your calling will be tested, but continue to walk toward your destiny, toward the fulfillment of His great calling on your life.

Chapter Two

The Most Essential Step

The Most Essential Step

Let me tell you right upfront that you cannot do it. It's impossible for you to change the world. Now you may wonder what the rest of the book is all about, but I encourage you to read on and find out what the solution to this mystery is.

Yes, you can positively (as well as negatively) affect the world around you, but is it going to make a difference in the long run? Is it going to make an *eternal* difference? There are many good people around the world who do great humanitarian work, helping to alleviate human suffering where it is very great and unbearable to watch. But does it really make a difference if you help a poor person improve his life, yet he will spend eternity separated from the God who created and loved him? What difference have you made from an eternal perspective?

All your wonderful works, all your deeds to help people, will count zero before the throne of God the day He judges you for your life on earth. He does not have a scale right beside the judgment seat to see whether your good deeds outweigh the bad ones. Even if you have only ever done one bad thing in all your life, your judgment will be eternal damnation and separation from God (see Rom. 6:23). Now you may think that is mean and unfair—but let me tell you a story.

Guilty

A young man was caught stealing food in the grocery store and had to appear before a judge for his crime. This young man had been a model citizen up to that point, working hard, paying his taxes, and helping others. He was loved and appreciated by everyone who knew him. When he appeared in front of the judge, he explained the dire situation he was in, which had forced him to steal food from the store. It had been an act of sheer desperation. The judge felt sorry for the young man, but he had the law to uphold. The judge had only one choice—to pronounce the young man guilty of stealing. The gavel came down as the guilty verdict was announced.

Likewise, each one of us would be pronounced guilty by God for the many things we have done in our lives. God makes sure we are aware of that when He says that there is no person who has not sinned (see 1 John 1:8), and we are painfully aware of that as we live with the bad choices we have made in our lives, the things we would undo if at all possible. It looks hopeless as we live under the curse that came into the world with Adam's fall.

But then, GOD. God is love. God longs for a relationship with His masterpiece creation, the ones He created in His own image. His heart was broken when Adam turned away from Him, and it's broken with every person who chooses not to be in relationship with Him. But is there a way to be in relationship with Him? I thought Adam made that impossible.

> *Therefore, just as sin entered the world through one man, and death through sin, and in this way death came to all men, because all sinned. …how much more will those who receive God's abundant provision of grace and of the gift of righteousness reign in life through the one Man, Jesus Christ! Consequently, just as one trespass resulted in condemnation for all people, so also **one righteous act resulted in justification and life for all people**. For just as through the disobedience of the one man the many were made sinners, so also through the obedience of the one Man the many will be made righteous* (Romans 5:12,17-19).

For as in Adam all die, so in Christ all will be made alive
(1 Corinthians 15:22).

What is the apostle Paul talking about in these two Scripture passages? Jesus is called the "last Adam" in God's Word (see 1 Cor. 15:45). Jesus came to undo the damage Adam brought. How is that possible?

God's heart was broken when He lost His relationship with man and woman, and He knew there was only one way to restore His original plan of complete union between Him and His prized creation. Somebody had to take the punishment of death upon Himself, therefore freeing humankind. Since no human is without sin, that was not an option. There is only One who is without sin—God Himself. So the all-powerful, almighty God chose to lower Himself, to restrict Himself to a human body, to humble Himself and become a lowly human baby, helpless, and dependent on others (see Phil. 2:6-8). Jesus was born to the virgin Mary, conceived by Holy Spirit, over 2,000 years ago. God had become Man, had become His own creation. What a miracle, what a mystery!

A Sinless Life

Jesus lived a sinless life—the only one who ever did—giving us a great example of how to live, and showing us the nature of our heavenly Father, and then He did the unthinkable. He chose to take our punishment upon Himself and allowed Himself to be arrested and condemned to death on a cross. His love for us, His longing for relationship with us was so great, that He was ready to go to the utmost extreme for its restoration.

We get a glimpse of Jesus' heart as He kneels, weeping in Jerusalem saying:

O Jerusalem, Jerusalem, you who kill the prophets and stone those sent to you, how often I have longed to gather your children together, as a hen gathers her chicks under her wings, but you were not willing (Matthew 23:37, Luke 13:34).

Yet while we wanted nothing to do with Him, He went to the cross anyway, He died anyway. It was His love for us that held Him to the cross. It was the anticipated joy of having a beautiful Bride that held the Bridegroom to the cross (see Heb. 12:2). He looked at each one of us and said, *You are worth it. I'm doing this for you. I love you so much, I long so much for relationship with you. I want you to be My friend, My child, My lover. Will you accept My sacrifice for you?*

The sun disappeared and darkness covered the earth for hours as Jesus was dying. He was disfigured beyond recognition from all the beatings, yet all He could feel was the joy of accomplishing His destiny, of completing the most crucial act of all history. Soon, very soon, the suffering would be over, and it would have been so worth it. And He breathed His last, saying, "It is finished" (John 19:30). Jesus had taken the sin of humanity upon Himself, the sin of every human being who had ever lived and who would ever live. He died for you and for me. He made the greatest sacrifice anyone could ever make—dying for another person (see John 15:13). Not only that, but He died for us before He even knew whether we would accept His sacrifice. What great love!

Not to Condemn but to Save

Many years ago I heard the following story that still breaks my heart every time I hear it.

There was once a father whose wife had died and all he had left was his young son whom he loved more than anything in his world. This father had a unique job. He worked in a small booth by a train bridge, his only task was to open the bridge when a ship was approaching, and lower it when a train was coming. He had a set schedule, and so it was not a difficult job to do. One day, he saw the train approaching and was going to lower the bridge as usual. Then he realized in total shock that his son was climbing around the hydraulics of the bridge. If he lowered the bridge, he would kill his own son. What should he do? Keep the bridge open, save his son, and cause a train derailment that could kill hundreds, or lower the bridge and save the hundreds at the cost of his son? He was in agony as he slowly moved the lever to the closed position, killing his only beloved son, and saving the people on the train. What a sacrifice this father made!

Still, this story pales compared to what our heavenly Father did for us when He allowed His Son, Jesus, to be tortured and killed a most cruel death on a cross. Yet the pain was mixed with joy. Three days later Jesus came back to life! He was resurrected to life with a new glorified body, having gained victory over sin and death, and having opened the door for every human being to be in relationship with God again. The veil in the temple that separated God's presence and His people was torn. The first Adam's deed was undone. The last Adam had accomplished it at a great price.

> *For God so loved the world that He gave His one and only Son, that whoever believes in Him shall not perish but have eternal life. For God did not send His Son into the world to condemn the world, but to save the world through Him* (John 3:16-17).

As soon as the guilty verdict was announced, Jesus entered the room and took the young man's place. "You can go. I will take care of it. I will bear your penalty, because I love you so much. Accept My gift for you, My beloved." In tears the young man walked away, his eyes locked with Jesus' eyes of love, unable to look away. He felt humbled, unworthy, and so very grateful. Thanks to Jesus' great sacrifice on the cross, we go free. We can enter a relationship with the Creator of the universe, enter into His presence, and enter into an eternity in perfect union with Him.

Home Life and School Life

I started my relationship with God at the age of 20. All my life I had been looking for love, had been longing to be loved and have someone who cared. I had no clue there was a God of love out there who wanted me more than I wanted what He had to offer.

I grew up in a nominal Catholic home, like most people in Austria. As long as I can remember I believed there was a God, but nobody ever told me you could know Him personally. My dad left us gradually when I was around five years old, and my mom was alone for seven years with me and my younger brother. She was glad to have help from her parents who we spent a lot of time with while we were growing up.

When I was 12 years of age, my mom's boyfriend moved in with us, and the years of darkness started for me. I became depressed, wanting to either kill him or myself, and was crying myself to sleep every night, crying out to an unknown God in case He could hear me.

In school, I loved religious instruction and finding out more about God. At times I went to Mass on Sundays, and I found some comfort in that, but it never lasted for long. My one goal as a teenager was to find a boyfriend who would give me the love I so craved, but I was unsuccessful. I was actually somewhat of an outsider in my class and felt like I was the only person in the world. At times I thought that the world would be better off without me. I was hoping that my death would make Mom come to her senses so she'd leave her boyfriend. But I never had the courage to even try to commit suicide.

A few things kept me from doing so; one, I knew God would not like it, and two, I did not want to miss out on what was ahead and always had a little hope that things would get better. If only someone had told me the awesome news of this loving God who held His hands over me the first twenty years of my life, protecting me in situations of physical, sexual, and emotional abuse. If only I had known I could fall into His loving arms and experience the fullness of life that can only be found in Him. Instead, I struggled on.

When I graduated from high school at the age of 18, there was no more religious instruction, and no more thoughts of God. I attended the university and slowly started to get a grip on life. Life was getting a little better, bit by bit, and I was content.

But God had not forgotten my tears. He had not forgotten my many prayers crying out to Him. He had not forgotten the longing in my heart to know Him. All along my journey through life, He was excited about the wonderful destiny He had planned for me, the awesome things He had prepared for me, His little princess, His precious chosen one, His beloved daughter.

And in 1993, He decided it was time. I can imagine His excitement as He anticipated the day I would finally meet Him in person. And so He set everything in place for this most important day of my life.

Summer break was approaching, and I wanted to attend a week-long tennis camp organized by the student union at the university, which I had attended before. However, it was too expensive for me, so I was looking for alternatives. My friend and tennis partner found a folder explaining about a sports camp organized by a Christian student group, and threw it away. However, she told me it was much cheaper, and so I asked her to get it out of the trash. In Austria, a catholic country, everything is called Christian, so it didn't bother me. The deadline was past, but they let us sign up anyway. A boy who was pursuing my friend signed up as well.

At the camp there were nightly teachings on the subject of relationships, and the first night my friend and I went to check it out, and liked it. We had arrived late and didn't realize that there had been singing and prayer beforehand. We liked what we heard and decided to attend again the next day.

The following night, I was on time and found a seat, reserving one for my friend right next to me. I waited and waited, but she didn't show up. I got nervous when the singing started, and then the praying—I felt very uncomfortable in the midst of all those "saints." I kept wondering where my friend was and was getting angry at her for abandoning me. I was scared to get up and leave, but finally I did. Fuming, I went to my room, waiting for my friend who had been out with a boy who had been pursuing her.

I decided to stop talking to her until she apologized. My mother used that method to punish me while growing up. Needless to say, I became very miserable being all alone with these "weird" people, while my friend enjoyed being with that boy. Finally I decided to make the most of the remaining week at camp.

One night at dinner I overheard a young man sharing how he had come to know the Lord a few months earlier, and it awakened my curiosity. I asked him to tell me more and as he did, I felt my face getting warm and radiating; I was soaking up every word he was saying. Later that evening, there was a talent night and the students were performing skits, games, and songs. One song was called, "It's Your Own Choice."

The words were about Jesus and how we have a choice to make. That song pierced me through and through.

I wanted to choose to follow Jesus, but I knew that I had to reconcile with my friend first. So the following morning I took the difficult step of asking her to be friends again, and it took a few days before our relationship was restored. But that night—July 15, 1993—I was lying in bed with tears running down my face, and I thanked God for having me brought to the camp. I asked Him to never leave my life again. The following morning, I woke up a new person.

> *Therefore, if anyone is in Christ, the new creation has come: the old has gone, the new is here* (2 Corinthians 5:17).

I was full of joy, love, and peace, feeling like I was on cloud nine. It was astounding. People around me noticed.

Born Again!

I returned to Vienna a little apprehensive. What if it was just the camp environment? What if it was just temporary? Was what I was feeling real? I was also dreading encountering my family again. But I was born from above, born again (see John 3). The God of creation had come to live inside of me. He had given me true life, life in abundance (see John 10:10). I had become a child of God, had entered into a relationship with my Friend, Jesus, my Bridegroom, my Lover, my Lord, my Savior, my Brother, He who is Love, who is Life, who is Light, who is Peace, who is the Way, the Resurrection, the Bread of God.

> *Everyone who calls on the name of the Lord will be saved* (Romans 10:13).

I had called upon His name and had found salvation. The Greek word for "saved" encompasses health for body, soul, and mind, forgiveness of sin, and prosperity; salvation for every aspect of our lives. I was a new baby in God's Kingdom, and it showed. Within one hour, my parents (my mother and step-father) asked what had happened to me. They saw the book, *Following Jesus*, I was reading, and they didn't like it.

In Austria, the Catholic church is the only church. There are a few Lutheran churches that are frowned upon, and every other church is considered a cult. So my family was really concerned that I had fallen prey to a cult, especially when I went to church two days in a row. But God had done the most awesome miracle in my life. The man I had hated so much, who I felt had stolen my teenage years, I now had love for. Love that I had no ability to produce but that flowed from Heaven straight to me. I showered that love on him and Mom as the days went by and left him speechless at least once during that time.

True Love

The honeymoon went on for weeks. My first act was to get a Bible, and I could not stop reading as tears flowed down my face at the wonderful things I read. I was in love, truly in love for the first time in my life, and my Lover was there to stay, there to love me unconditionally for the rest of my life, there to protect me, lead me, heal me, restore me, and transform me more and more into His image, from glory to glory, entering more and more into the fullness He promised us even this side of Heaven.

Almighty God chose me even before the foundation of the world. He formed me in my mother's womb (see Ps. 139:13). He had a great plan for me (see Jer. 29:11). He called me to be a world changer, to carry the Gospel of the Kingdom to the ends of the earth, to be His hands, feet, ears, eyes, and mouth on this earth. He called me to be an ambassador for His heavenly Kingdom, a reflection of who He is so the world would meet Him and turn to Him, so Heaven would be populated and hell be emptied.

The Lord had chosen a nobody, a despised, lowly, thrown away, discarded, broken little girl who had nothing to offer at all (see 1 Cor. 1:28), and He said, *Give her to Me and let the world see that nothing is impossible for God.* And so, all those years ago, in 1993, He took this broken, ugly vessel and started the process of restoration, beautification, and equipping, so that the vessel could be used again for its purpose and intention rather than being thrown into the trash. The world said, "Impossible." God said, "Possible." And guess who was right?

Vessel of Honor

There is no vessel too broken, no vessel too ugly, that the Master Potter cannot restore it and make it into a vessel of honor for His glory. Just come to Him. Just dare to trust this God of love, even though you've never had reason to trust anyone in your life. Take the risk, and you will not be disappointed. Offer Him the broken pieces of your life, and watch what He can do.

You can't do it yourself, though you've tried so many times. Other people can't give you what you need, though you thought they could over and over and were disappointed again and again. What do you have to lose? You have nothing to lose and everything to gain. Just lift your voice to your heavenly Father whose arms are outstretched toward you. See His eyes of love and the tears of longing for you to come running to Him, jump into His arms, and let Him embrace you and wash away your tears, sorrow, and pain and love you back to life. Read the following prayer out loud and start your new, wonderful life.

~

Heavenly Father, I believe that You love me and desire me as part of Your family. I believe that You sacrificed Your Son Jesus out of love for me. I believe that Jesus is God who became man to reveal Yourself to me. I confess that I have sinned, that I deserve eternal punishment and that I need a Savior. I believe that Jesus died for me on the cross, and that He rose again. I accept Jesus' sacrifice and ask You to forgive me all my sin. Wash me completely clean. I choose to follow You the rest of my life. I want You to be my Lord and Savior, my Brother and Friend, my Bridegroom and Lover. Fill me with Your Holy Spirit right now, with Your love, peace, and joy. Thank You for transforming me into Your image day by day. I want to know You more and more, and I thank You for the great plan You have for my life. I love You and praise and adore You. Amen.

Change Points

1. All your wonderful works, all your deeds to help people, will count zero before the throne of God the day He judges you for your life on earth.

2. Jesus was resurrected to life with a new glorified body, having gained victory over sin and death, and having opened the door for every human being to be in relationship with God again.

3. Moment by moment, you can fall into His loving arms and experience the fullness of life that can only be found in Him.

4. God will protect you, lead you, heal you, restore you, and transform you more and more into His image, from glory to glory, entering more and more into the fullness He promised you even this side of Heaven.

5. Trust the God of love, even though you may have never had reason to trust anyone in your life. Let Him embrace you, and He will wash away your tears, sorrow, and pain.

Chapter Three

Discovering and Pursuing Your Destiny

Discovering and Pursuing Your Destiny

Now that you have taken the most essential step and made the most important decision of your life, now that you are a son, a daughter, of the Most High God, the Creator of the universe, you have started on the road toward your destiny. You have chosen the narrow path (see Matt. 7:14), you have started the race (see 1 Cor. 9:24), you have started the wonderful journey of being transformed into the likeness of Jesus from glory to glory (2 Cor. 3:18), walking hand in hand with your awesome heavenly Father on the road to fulfillment, to perfection, to being complete and perfect once you stand in Heaven face to face with your Beloved.

Avoid Distractions

On this road, there are many distractions; there are enemies, disasters, painful things, and temptations. It will be easy for you to look away from your Father whose hand you are holding. But fix your eyes on Him always (see Heb. 12:2). Don't fix your eyes on the enemy, on the problem, or on the barrier blocking the road. While it may be totally dark around you, you are safe holding His hand (see Ps. 23:4, 139:12). In fact, there is no safer place to be.

Yes, the wide road looks so beautiful, so easy, with lots of light; but remember, satan is an angel of light (2 Cor. 11:14). Believe me, while the road might be beautiful and easy, you do not want to reach its destination. Trust your Father; trust He is leading you down the right path. Don't let go of His hand and veer off the right, narrow path.

God has prepared many good things for you on this journey (see Jer. 29:11). He has promised joy, peace, and love on the way—but He never promised that it would be an easy journey. No, we were promised that we would have troubles on this journey (see John 16:33), but that He would never ever leave us or forsake us. He will never let go of our hands. He will always hold on tight and not allow the enemy to tear us away from Him. With Him is the safest place in the whole universe.

Gaze upon His face, look into His eyes of love, and the world around you will fade away. Problems will seem small, not worth looking at. He knows what you need, and He knows the solution to each one of your problems. He does not want you to rattle off a list of needs whenever you approach Him. He wants a lover. He wants you to spend time with Him, just to be with Him. When you are in love, you just want cuddle and sometimes you don't talk for the longest time, as no words are needed. That's what He wants—lovers, friends, not mere servants and subjects, though that's what we are as well.

And once you are walking on this road with your Father, hand in hand, He will lower His face to your ear from time to time and whisper things to you. As you walk on with Him, He will let you know of things ahead, of things He wants you to do. You will never have the complete picture because He knows how much information about the road ahead you can handle at the time. He wants you to simply trust Him, trust He has your best interests in mind. Trust that everything that is going to happen will work out for your good at the end (see Rom. 8:28), even if the enemy is the one who caused the mess. I am continually blown away how God is able to take the greatest tragedies and make good things come out of them. That is our God!

While on this path with Him, He directs you toward your destiny from the very beginning, though you might not recognize it at the time. Some things seem coincidental, others seem so insignificant that you don't even realize their importance until much later.

My Journey

When I started my life with Jesus in the summer of 1993, everything was already set in place for me to go to Paris for half a year to study, and I left Austria just over a month after my birthday. I believe that the Lord had arranged this trip even before I ever said yes to Him. That half-year in Paris was very significant for many reasons. It is where God revived my love for the French language, which I had had all my life. Obviously God knew that He would be sending me to French-speaking Africa. He called me to Africa in the months after I heard a missionary from Africa speak. This is where He baptized me in His Spirit, while I had no clue what was going on. And now I know it was no coincidence that that happened in a healing seminar.

God also knew that I needed to be away from my family who was dysfunctional and against my newfound faith, and so I was able to flourish and grow rapidly as a new believer. Paris is also where God called me to full-time ministry only two months after I had come to the Lord. I remember Holy Spirit's intense stirring in my heart, as I felt so deeply that nothing but serving God wholly was worth doing. All I wanted was to serve Him with every word, action, and minute of my day. When I shared how I felt with one of my leaders there, I was told this feeling would go away; I was just a young believer.

Well, it didn't.

I had such a hunger for God's Word. I thought that I could not possibly call myself a Christian without having read the whole Bible, so I read and read, including the whole apocrypha as all I had was my old Catholic school Bible. I was simply ignorant, but I accomplished my goal after five months.

A Dream

Just a little while later, I had a dream that impacted me profoundly. At that time I had been asking God for direction. My double-major at the university was in astronomy and physics, and I had come to Paris to do an astronomy internship, which did not work out, so I took a few physics classes. In school, my emphasis had been on languages, not mathematics, and so I had always struggled with math at the college level—cheating my way through all my math classes. As a believer, I could not do that any more, and I came to the realization that I was in academic trouble.

That night I had a dream and in the dream was asked whether I had ever considered going to Bible school. The question baffled me in the dream, and would not let me go during the days ahead. God had put the dream of going to Bible school into my heart. I decided to pursue that desire, and during the summer I visited several Bible schools in England. Unfortunately the entrance requirements included being a believer for three years before enrollment, and I was only a one-year-old believer at the time. My time had not come yet.

A few years later, I heard Mike Bickle teach at a conference in Switzerland and was profoundly impacted. His teaching presented a major paradigm shift in the way I understood my relationship with God; and during the following ministry time, I had an awesome vision of Jesus as my Bridegroom. When I found out more about Mike Bickle's school in Kansas City, Missouri—teaching the bridal paradigm, the prophetic, and worship—my heart was longing to go there and be formed there. The desire was so great that during the following years, I requested the school's new catalogue a few times, always dreaming that I could go there. Even though other things were happening in my life, the longing to go to Bible school remained.

When I finished my studies in Austria in 2000, the question returned. Could I go to Bible school now? Yes, the time had come! In 2001, I finally started Bible school—seven and a half years after God had put that desire in my heart.

Your Heart's Desire

If you are wondering what your destiny is, what your calling is, then ask yourself, for what do I have a passion? What breaks my heart? What do I love doing most? It is the Lord who puts the desire in your heart, to direct you toward your destiny; and He is also the One who will give you your heart's desire as long as you stay at His hand and delight in Him more than anything else (see Ps. 37:4).

As a little girl, even before I went to school, I loved playing school. My poor little brother had to be my student. Imagine a 5-year-old being the teacher with a 2-year-old student! Later, I even developed sophisticated curriculum and tried to use them on my brother who wasn't as willing any more. In my late teens, I wanted to open a "dance club." Ballroom dancing, Rock'n'Roll (acrobatics), and tap dance were my life, and I even trained for competitions at one point. I loved dancing and teaching, and so I was starting this club to pass on my knowledge. When too many older people and "weirdoes" wanted to join, I got cold feet and abandoned my plans.

At the age of 15, I started tutoring English and math, and continued until I left Austria at the age of 28. During those 13 years, I taught English, math, French, and a little German, and I loved it with a passion. God had given me a unique ability to help my students grasp concepts, even the most challenging ones. And during times of darkness, depression, and discouragement, teaching would always lift my spirit and restore my joy. That's what it means to be called to something!

At the age of 24, I attended a three-week intense course from Cambridge University to become a certified English teacher. I was the only non-native speaker, and not only did I graduate, but I graduated top of my class with an above average grade. I had enjoyed every minute of the intense three weeks. Thanks to that certificate, I also started teaching at language schools at night—another source of joy. My private students as well as the language schools allowed me to finance my studies as my only income besides funds from my father. At my church, I started a tutoring club. Once a week, we helped children for free; it was a great way to take away their fear of going into a church building, and opened doors for them to hear the gospel—several children came to know the Lord.

Was all this my purpose in life? It is beyond doubt that God has given me an ability and passion for teaching even as He created me in my mother's womb. All those years of teaching bore fruit at the time—joy for me, and success for my students—but it also foreshadowed my calling.

Natural, God-given Talents

At the end of my studies when I was wondering how to get into the country of Mali in West Africa, I was not even thinking of going there to teach until I talked to another missionary lady. I went online and found two schools in Bamako, the capital of Mali—a big, official French school, and a small, Muslim school. I emailed both schools, and received no reply from the first, and an immediate reply from the second. "Come teach German, school starts October 1." The day this Macedonian call reached me was my tenth birthday in the Lord to the day.

All those years of teaching had prepared me to go to Mali as a German teacher in the most challenging setting imaginable. I had 70 students in one class, most of whom did not care to learn German at all, and who took full advantage of this greenhorn in their culture who did not know the way things worked there. But I was in my element doing what I loved most, and so I was able to work out the challenges and keep going for two full years. Today, I teach the rescued children from the streets of Mali—not only in Bible school, but I teach my children English and teach our children who spend the night on our base to read and write. Those are some of my favorite times of all!

God has given us all natural talents. If it is God who has given them to us, then don't you think He had a purpose in doing so? What are you good at? What do you love doing? Where could you go from where you are now to use your talent for God's glory?

Another talent that runs in our family is music. My grandfather was a professor at the music conservatory in Vienna where people from around the world go to study. He was part of the Vienna Philharmonic Orchestra and played the viola in the opera house, for the annual New Year's concert, and traveled the world with them. As a little kid, I taught myself to play the recorder, and was then sent to music school for two years where I became very proficient on it, playing classical music. When in fifth grade, I started attending an upper class music school learning piano, where we had to take exams and perform in concerts. I had to practice for an hour every day, and my grandfather was very strict as he made sure we did our piano homework and could play the pieces. After four years at this very reputable music school, I could play difficult classical pieces.

However, the pressure was too intense for me, and I quit, refusing to touch the piano for many years, except at Christmas time.

A few years later, I had a few classical guitar lessons. When I became a believer, I had a desire to play the guitar for worship, and so I taught myself. Soon I was able to sing worship songs with my guitar. But my passion was with the piano, and I was overjoyed when I was able to purchase an electronic piano at great savings. I started worshiping the Lord with it, lifting my spirit and entering into His presence. I also took piano and singing lessons for a short time. I once led a choir for a special event, and I joined the worship team at my church as a singer. I loved singing, and sang a few special songs at church or church events over the years.

While in Kansas City where I found the intimacy with God I had always longed for, leading worship took on a whole new dimension. As I lived in His presence and glory, coming into His throne room, I would take people along with me. Today the most precious times we have in Mali are when I sit down at the piano. We start worshiping God, and the heavens open up, and His glory comes down. We get lost in His presence, enveloped by His love and beauty, and we cannot help but worship and worship, forgetting all time. There is nothing that I love more today—whether in Mali, Austria, or America—than sitting down at the piano and being ushered into His presence together with everyone who is there. That is where there is joy, healing, restoration, and anything we need. What a privilege to lead others to the throne this way!

God takes our natural abilities, and as He breathes on them, we are able to go to a new level, using them to their full capacity and for what they were intended—God's glory and honor and purposes!

New Desires and Talents

Besides using our natural abilities that He has placed in us when He created us, God is also able to completely rewire us and give us new desires and talents we never in the least had in our lives. Growing up, I never ever even thought of Africa, and I certainly had no desire to ever go there. Except for the times I would urge my little brother to play school with me, I also had no interest in children—or teaching them—and didn't care for them at all. It is ironic that during the ten years I was a believer before going to Africa, I never ever served in children's ministry in church, while I had done every other ministry imaginable. Today, children are at the center of what I do and love doing. How is that possible?

In 1997 a short, eight-minute report came on television. It was about the street children in the capital of Mali. As I was watching, my heart was breaking and I broke into tears over these abandoned, forgotten, hopeless children without a future. I cried to God to use me to make a difference. Years later He answered that prayer.

The first time the Lord gave me a true love for children was during my first time in Mali in 1999 when I lived with a missionary family for two months. They had three little kids who became very dear to me. Something changed in my heart during that time.

The final piece in this process of preparation fell into place in November 2002 while I was in Kansas City. I took a prophetic class, and on the last day of that class, the speaker, Kim Terrell, and his friend, were praying and prophesying over every student. Even before they started praying for me, God's Spirit was already profoundly upon me. While they were praying and prophesying, I was trembling and going to a very deep place in God. I was glad that the word was recorded as I might not have remembered much at all.

While this prophetic word was important for more than one reason as I will share later, something very significant happened that day. I have never received a word like that before or since. It felt like there was actual creative power in the words spoken. God was using them and changing me in the innermost part of my being. The last part of the word was, "The Lord is gonna put you in a place where you may end up ministering; you're ministering to children. I see you doing things with kids, on an extreme level. I see kids getting purity, total purity, of what the word is about, through the words the Lord gives you to speak."

Suddenly, whenever I opened my Bible, I saw children. Suddenly, everywhere I looked were children. Suddenly, I had a consuming love for children like I had never had before. God had rewired me and steered me toward His great plans to use me for His glory.

~

Lord, thank You for the many talents You have given me. Please help me to discover them all and develop them so they can be used for Your glory. Thank You for giving me all the additional talents and abilities I need to fulfill Your great calling on my life. Thank You for placing Your heart's desire into my heart and making it a reality. Thank You that You always provide a solution in times of trouble, temptation, pain, and distraction. I choose to always keep my eyes on You and walk on into my destiny. Hallelujah!

Change Points

1. On the road to fulfilling your God-given destiny, there are many distractions; there are enemies, disasters, painful things, and temptations.

2. You will have troubles on your life journey (see John 16:33), but He will never ever leave you or forsake you. He will never let go of your hand.

3. During times of darkness, depression, and discouragement, your God-given passion will lift your spirit and restore your joy. That's what it means to be called to something!

4. In addition to using your natural abilities that He placed in you, God is also able to completely rewire you and give you new desires and talents that you never even imagined.

5. God will use His purpose and love for you to change the innermost part of your being for good.

Chapter Four

Called Away

Called Away

Now you're probably wondering, *But how did you end up in Mali? How did you know He was sending you there? How did you find out you were called to Africa?*

Even growing up I was always interested in how things work and in making new discoveries. While other girls wanted Barbies for their birthdays, I wanted a chemistry kit or an electronics kit. As a teenager, I had a subscription to a science magazine, and I devoured it. I was also fascinated with languages ever since I was a little girl. For many years I wanted to become an interpreter or translator. I learned three foreign languages in high school. But in 9th grade, I made a shift to science. I had a dreadful English teacher and lost my love for that language, but I really liked physics—and French.

I started reading pseudo-scientific books on astronomy and lost my heart to that field. I totally shifted from languages to science, and when I finished high school, it was clear that I would study astronomy and physics at the university. For quite a few years I was involved at an observatory in Vienna where I was even part of the executive committee for a while as an administrator. I assisted in guided tours at night, showing stars and nebulae to people, and I loved it.

But what I loved most was knowing that there was so much yet to be discovered, so much unknown. At that time, I was dreaming of getting the Nobel Prize one day for a great discovery I would make. Even then I dreamed big! Even then I wanted to venture into the unknown where no one had gone before. God had put that into me, knowing what He had prepared for me. And when I decided to live with Him and for Him only, the true intention of that facet of my nature was redeemed. It came to life in my spirit as well, and as God prepared me to step into my destiny, He formed, adjusted, and put into the right place my desire for the unknown, making it precious to be used for His glory alone.

Life With My Beloved

From the moment I started my life with my Beloved, I had a passion to make Him known to all the people around me. Two weeks after that day, I wrote my testimony about how I had come to the Lord (you can find it on my Website) and gave it to every person I knew, whether mailing it to them or putting it into their hands. Just over a week after my new birth, I was out in the streets evangelizing for the first time. Oh how I longed to pass on this good news I had only just found myself! There is a God who loves you and wants you to know Him! Hallelujah!

It did not take long before God started breaking my heart for my family, for my city and country, and even for the ends of the earth. There were times I would take the subway or bus, and all I could see were people in pain and in need of Jesus, people going to hell, people who needed to hear the good news. Every time I walked by a beggar, my heart would go out to him, and I wished I could do something. In 1994, I watched a few documentaries on different cults, and all I could do was weep for these people who were so deceived. I watched several videos on unreached peoples that Wycliffe Bible Translators had produced, and my heart broke every time. Seeing these realities rendered me speechless, having to go off by myself and find the face of the Lord, bringing those people before His throne with groaning and weeping. My whole being was pierced with the pain of people going to hell, of not knowing Jesus, or not even having a chance to find out about Jesus. Every tear running down my face, every groan uttered, was a prayer of intercession for the lost, for the unreached, for those who are perishing. Countless times I had to go before my Creator, my Savior, my Redeemer after watching some program, because I was unable to understand how other people watching did not feel the same way. Why weren't we all on the floor crying out to God for these precious people He loved and created, but were dying without Him?

Send Me!

One day I heard a real story that deeply pierced my heart. A missionary went to South America and went to a remote village and preached the gospel to the people there. They received it with joy, and the whole village decided to follow Jesus. In the midst of the excitement, the village chief was curious and asked the missionary, "Tell me, how long ago did Jesus do this for us?"

The missionary replied, "Two thousand years ago."

The village chief was in shock and unbelief as he responded, "Do you mean, it took you two thousand years to bring us this great news? What took you so long?"

The pain pierced me through and through. We have had this good news for 2,000 years, and yet there are thousands and millions of people who have never heard it. Every day people are searching for God, and no one is there to tell them how to find Him, and so they die without Him, going to an eternity without Him.

There was only one way I could respond, with tears running down and sobs coming from the depth of my being. "Lord, here I am, send me! Lord, send me where they have never heard the good news. Send me where nobody wants to go! I will go for You, wherever it is, however hard it is, I don't care. Take me, use me, make me Your mouthpiece, make me Your hands and feet. Let me bring the good news to the ends of the earth!"

I cannot tell you how many times I have prayed this prayer the first ten years of my Christian life before I finally got to go. The Lord heard my heart's cry, which was really His heart's cry, and He accepted my offer and started putting things in place. He started reordering steps, moving things around, directing what only He can in the invisible world, to create divine appointments, divine encounters, and divine coincidences. He revived my love for the French language in Paris and broke my heart for Africa when I heard a missionary share about her life there. He directed my eyes and heart toward French-speaking Africa, and gave me His heart, pulling me in that direction with a divine pull I could not resist. I knew that He was calling me there.

However, it was two years after my new birth that God finally specified the country of Mali. I had a few countries on my heart for which I had spent much time interceding. I had finally given up finishing my studies of astronomy and physics, and was content with my Bachelor's degree. I met a girl whose major was African studies, and was amazed that even existed. After much prayer for direction, I knew that African studies was to be my new major, with French as my minor. Yes, I wanted to go to Bible school, but I believed that these studies would also uniquely prepare me for God's calling.

My biggest disappointment was that starting over with my studies would mean so many more years before actually going to the mission field. I truly felt that Jesus might come back before I could actually go to Africa and tell them about Him. During all those years, I was in constant tension of longing more than anything to be in the place where God had called me, but it was not to be yet. I had to learn patience and perseverance as He prepared me.

Preparation

It was the summer of 1995, just as I was about to start my new African studies classes when I was suddenly confronted with Mali over and over again. I sent a donation to Wycliffe Bible translators, and they passed it on to a missionary in Mali who wrote me a letter. When I looked at the choice of three languages as my first language at the university, Bambara—the main language of Mali—was one of the three. But most of all, God started breaking my heart for the people of Mali. He showed them to me, and all I could do was weep and intercede for them.

When I started my studies in the fall, I knew God was calling me to Mali, and so everything I did was focused on Mali wherever I had a choice. I had to learn history and literature and politics, but my focus was on linguistics. And so I prepared practically, learning two Malian languages and analyzing a third one for my Master's thesis. I got to know the precious people in Mali through what I learned and what the Lord showed me, and my longing to be there grew. When, oh Lord, when would I go?

Fours years after He called me to Mali, the time had finally come. In 1999 I went to Mali to conduct linguistic research for my thesis for five months. As soon as I stepped off the plane, I knew I was home. I was where I belonged. I had no culture shock; everything seemed familiar. After all, I had already been there many times in the spirit, during intercession. I loved every minute of my time there, though I worked very hard and had quite a few challenges to conquer.

God directed my steps, knowing which experiences were crucial for me so He could guide me in the direction He had for me when I would return to Mali to stay. One time the missionaries I was with and I approached the house of one of their workers. The wife was the most joyful lady I had met in the whole village, but that day all I could see on her face was sheer terror. There was also a big crowd of people gathered around the tree by their house. We found out that two owls had taken up residence in the tree, and that owls were the ones with contact to the underworld. The wife was close to giving birth to her child, and she was convinced that the owls had come to steal her baby's soul. Oh how my heart was breaking for this woman! I wanted to tell her of Jesus, and that she had no reason to be afraid. I encouraged the missionaries to speak to her, but Jesus' name was never uttered that day. I was broken on the inside.

Another time I went with another missionary to his village, and people came with all their sicknesses, and the missionary only gave them advice. Again, I never heard the name of Jesus. Oh how I longed to pray for all these people to be healed of their sicknesses!

On the whole, my idealism of what missionary life looked like was shattered. I was saddened to see many missionaries barely surviving, and certainly not thriving spiritually and having much fruit to show. I did and do not judge them, as the realities of missionary life are harsh.

When I boarded the plane to leave Mali and return to Austria, my heart was heavy having to leave "my" country. But I was also very serious as I said to the Lord, "There is no way I am going to be a dead missionary not making a difference. The only way I'm coming back to Mali is if You equip me with Your power to do what Jesus did."

Little did I know that that meant four more years of preparation. Years that were filled with more intercession and longing to finally return to my country. Today, I thank God that He took eight years to prepare me. Today, I know that I could not have gone even one month earlier. Do not despise the time of preparation, but make the most of it. I know that every tear I spilled for Mali counted in Heaven.

My Lost People

But there was another country I spilled a lot of tears for too—my own country of Austria. Every day I would see the pain and need and darkness in this nation that has more Muslims than Christians and the highest suicide rate in all of Europe. When I conducted a healing school in Canada in 1996, my reputation was that I had a passion for Austria. That's what the other students and teachers knew about me. Every time I was at a conference—mostly in other countries—I longed for people to remember Austria, not to forget this little country in the heart of Europe. I felt like an ambassador for Austria everywhere I went. I so longed to see a move of God in my nation. I longed to see revival. I longed for people to come to know Him and be saved. I spilled countless tears for the salvation of my nation, as I was overcome by God's heart for the lost people of Austria.

I did not remain inactive. I remember when I put a sandwich and tract together and laid it next to the beggar on the street who was sleeping by a vent in the middle of winter. And I came back to do it again. I alienated a lot of my friends in the early days when I witnessed like crazy to everyone wanting to know Jesus. The most damage was maybe done in my own family where I am to this day the only believer.

Oh how much time I have spent crying out to God for them! But all they could ever see was that I was "throwing away my life." They saw nothing but negative things, the positive changes in my life not counting for anything in their eyes. I will never forget the shock on my mom's face when I told her that I was getting baptized in water; of course, she did not come.

Since I got saved through the Christian student group, I got involved right away, and I went all out. I came back from the sports camp, and participated in the two-week evangelistic outreach the student group organized. I participated in Bible studies, evangelized, and talked to seekers. As soon as I arrived in Paris, I got involved with the student group there, and since my studies weren't working out as planned, I had plenty of time to work almost full-time with the student group. Four months after my conversion, I led my first Bible study. And I spent many hours evangelizing on the street with book tables and surveys, which was the way it was done back then. Returning to Austria, I became a leader within that Christian student organization and gave myself completely to it for two years. Not only did I grow rapidly, but God developed many of my giftings during that time of getting to use them on a smaller scale. Many people were on my heart who I witnessed to, whether once or repeatedly, and a few started a life with the Lord.

In 1996 I was introduced to "servant evangelism" for the first time, and it totally gripped me. I started a group within my church doing small acts of kindness for unbelievers. I loved sowing seeds of love by handing out cold drinks in traffic jams, milk and light bulbs on Sunday mornings when our stores are closed, as well as tissues in hay fever season or roses on Mother's Day. I had a passion for showing God's love to people out on the streets, those who would never come to church.

His Ambassador

While I was in Canada in 1996, Bill Bright's call went out to fast for 40 days for revival. Whole churches signed up to fast for 40 days in 1997, as did the church in Canada, and my heart was once again gripped, this time to fast for the salvation of my nation of Austria. I could not push away this desire and completed the 40-day fast for Austria in 1997. As you can imagine, my longing to see Austria saved only increased. When I finally left Austria for good in 2001 to continue preparing for my call to Africa, I asked the Lord, "What about Austria?" And I was comforted as He assured me that I would not miss His move in my beloved nation but would get to be part of it. Today I am so blessed, honored, and moved every time I return to my nation and get to be His ambassador as I preach, see the sick healed, and His glory come down in power to meet with His people.

God showed me His heart, and my heart responded in prayer and intercession. And my intercession opened the door for action, whether it meant others going in response to those prayers or myself. The prophets Ezra and Nehemiah (who were contemporaries) are great examples of this principle. They poured out their hearts in intercession, unable to do anything else. But God heard their prayers and sent them back to Jerusalem from their Babylonian captivity where they were able to rebuild the temple and city walls respectively.

For what is your heart breaking? What makes your heart burn with desire and passion? Has God shared His heart with you, whether it would be for a situation, a group of people or a certain kind of problem? Maybe you feel like there is nothing you can do to move into action in that direction. If so—pray! Allow Him to continue breaking your heart, allow Him to prepare you for the day when you will finally step out, step into what He has prepared for you. The higher your calling, the more difficult your calling, the longer your preparation, the deeper the dying you have to go through. Are you willing to pay the price? Are you willing to become someone who changes the world? Are you willing to be refined until you can shine with His glory—until there is nothing left of you, and all people see is Jesus in you?

I said yes to all these questions, and the Lord sovereignly sent me to Kansas City for two years where my life was completely changed once again. It was Heaven and it was hell, it was life and it was death, it was great and it was horrible, it was easy and it was hard. The Lord had put me into a pressure cooker, and the pressure was making this unseemly piece of coal into a beautiful diamond, though this coal did not like the pressure and the fire.

God had sent me to Kansas City after my academic preparation so He could answer the prayer that I would be equipped with His power to do what Jesus did. Mali was the reason I came to Kansas City, and it was continually before my eyes. When I did not like the pressure, I looked at the joy set before me, the Bride of Christ in Mali. When I went through hardship, I knew this was nothing compared to the hardship I would go through in Mali. And I counted it all joy as I went through suffering and trials (see James 1:2). OK, not always right away, but I knew it was all part of the preparation, part of the learning process, and I learned many lessons; many lessons we can only learn the hard way.

I continued interceding for Mali, continued longing to be there, while never forgetting my own nation of Austria either. As the two years in America were approaching their end, I was wondering how the huge vision for Mali God had given me over the years would ever come to pass. I had not even shared it with people as it seemed so crazy. But our God can do so much more than we could ever ask or imagine (see Eph. 3:20). I knew only God could bring a big vision like this to pass. If you are able to accomplish the vision you have, ask yourself whether it is really from God. God is the God of the impossible, the unimaginable, the incredible and outrageous! He loves showing off His greatness and stunning those who don't know Him to the point that they come running to Him.

Answered Prayer Ten Years Later

School finished the middle of May, and the next day was my 30th birthday. I felt great significance in that I started ministering at the same age Jesus started His ministry on earth. I wanted to start right, and really needed to know *how* to get started, so I decided to go on a 40-day fast leading up to my birthday. It was the most amazing 40 days! I was never hungry, never weak or tired. I was truly fed by God Himself from Heaven, and had a great time with Him. And most of all, a few weeks later He answered my prayer to open a door for me to go to Mali—in a most dramatic fashion.

I am someone who plans ahead, always trusting that God will direct my steps. He always has permission to change my direction at any time, and this is what God did. My plan was to return to Kansas City from Austria in July and stay in the United States the maximum time allowed without a visa, which was three months. The three months happened to end just at the time a church in Toronto had their "Catch the Fire" conference, and so I decided to attend that conference before going to Austria, and then fly to Mali for one month to see what doors God would open. Those were Claudia's plans.

Because of the conference, I was flying through Toronto to return to Austria, I was also flying into the U.S. via Toronto. For that reason I had to go through American immigration while still in Canada, before boarding my plane to Kansas City. I was worn out from ministering in Africa and Austria, and looking forward to returning home. While I was waiting in line for my turn, I noticed that one lady looked mean, and she ended up being my immigration officer. After some questions and looking into her computer, I was asked to follow her to a secure area where there were signs everywhere that I was being filmed. It was scary.

I had to sit down and wait for another grim officer who had me follow him into his little office. He told me that our conversation would be recorded and started asking me questions that I answered totally honestly. He knew that I had been allowed into the U.S. with an expired visa a year and a half earlier. He knew that I had tried to apply for a visa, but retracted my application because I thought that the school would be able to issue me a visa, which had never happened. In his eyes, I had broken the law, and he was convinced I was going to stay in Kansas City. I could not convince him otherwise. For that reason he told me I could not enter the United States of America. He told me that because they had made a mistake by letting me back into the U.S. previously, he would not put anything into the computer.

Though I was shocked by the news and felt like I was being treated like a criminal, I had the state of mind to ask when I could enter the U.S. again. He said that I could enter the next day if I could prove that I lived my life elsewhere, and not in the U.S. With that I was led outside.

I picked up my suitcase that they had retrieved from the plane, and there I was, stranded in Toronto. I was in shock. Tears were running down my face as I started to realize what had just happened. I felt lost and had no clue what to do next. I had no money.

Then I remembered that I had met some people who lived in Toronto during the missions trip to Africa, and I called one. She was so kind and picked me up from the airport and invited me to stay at her house for the night. But the nightmare was not over. I freaked out when she told me I could not stay there any longer than that. I did not know what to do as I had no money. I was so tired and just wanted to go home to Kansas City.

She arranged for me to rent a room with a Christian family, though I did not know how to pay for it, and dropped me off there. Unfortunately I did not feel I was welcome there either. Then I remembered another lady who was also in Toronto, and she said I could come stay with a woman in Toronto who had been an independent missionary in a country close to Mali. While talking with her, she shared a lot of helpful advice. I could possibly go to Mali as a teacher.

I went online to see whether there were any schools, and I found a big, French school, and a tiny Muslim Malian school. The director at the Malian school asked me to come teach German, with school starting in October. (I never heard back from the French school.)

It was July 15, 2003—exactly ten years to the day since my conversion. The Lord had given me the answer to my prayer for an open door on my tenth birthday.

I started gathering faxes and papers to prove to the immigration officer that I was not going to stay in the U.S., and rebooked my flight to Kansas City a few days later, a week after I had been turned away. I attended the conference at the church in Toronto, but could not really focus with so much at stake. Friends from Kansas City had come for the conference, and I was going to return to Kansas City on the same plane with them. I was so traumatized by the experience the previous week that I was terrified as we approached the immigration officers at Toronto airport. It was very early in the morning, and this time I noticed one immigration officer who looked very nice—and I ended up with her. She looked at all my papers, and in shock I watched her put the stamp of approval into my passport. I was crying as I walked away and again when I stepped onto the ground in Kansas City. I was back home! A few weeks later I got my doctorate, graduated, and left on a plane to Austria.

I met with the new senior pastor of my Austrian church, and was told they would think about supporting me. With no financial support, and no other person with me, I boarded a plane to Mali on September 18, 2003. As I stepped off that plane in Mali, I stepped into my destiny. I had come home. I was ready to walk at the hand of my big heavenly Daddy to fulfill His big dream for the nation and people of Mali.

Your Destiny

How can you find your own destiny? Think about what breaks your heart. Think about what you are passionate about. Allow God to instill His own heart into yours. Allow Him to direct your passion and heart toward what He has planned for you. Follow His leading as a little child who would trust his or her wonderful father. And as you go along in life, your destiny will become clearer and clearer.

Pursue it with all your heart, mind, and soul, as you pursue the Lover of your soul. Persevere, keep your eyes on the goal, be patient, and trust that He will not let you stray, but lead you toward your destination. If you are ready to start this journey, pray the following prayer with me:

> *Precious heavenly Father, I thank You for the awesome destiny You have for me. Thank You for Your great plan for me to make a difference in this world and for eternity. Thank You for revealing these plans to me step by step. Thank You for sharing Your heart with me and breaking my heart with that which breaks Your heart. Give me patience, endurance, and the joy of having the goal always in front of me, knowing the day will come when I will enter into my God-given destiny. Thank You for choosing me. Thank You for the honor of being Your representative on this earth. Amen.*

Change Points

1. God will form, adjust, and put into the right place your desire for the unknown, making it precious to be used for His glory alone.

2. Do not despise the time of preparation, but make the most of it.

3. If you want to start right, and really know *how* to get started, you may want to consider fasting.

4. Are you ready to walk at the hand of your big heavenly Daddy to fulfill His big dream for you?

5. Persevere, keep your eyes on the goal, be patient, and trust that He will not let you stray, but lead you toward your destination.

Chapter Five

God First

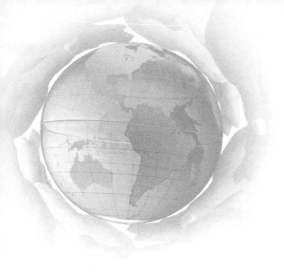

God First

When God tells us about something awesome He is going to do in our lives, when He shows us the wonderful things ahead, when we realize the great calling on our lives and the amazing destiny we have in God's Kingdom, we all want to enter into it right away, see its fulfillment right there and then. All I wanted during my ten years of preparation was to be in Mali, to be where God had called me, but the months and years just continued going by with me living in the tension of knowing my destiny and not having entered into it.

Patience

What do we learn during the preparation process? One key thing I had to learn was patience. Patience is a fruit of the spirit (see Gal. 5:22), which means it was deposited in us at our new birth, but it is up to us to water and develop it and see it grow. As we are transformed into His image more and more, the fruit of the spirit grows in our lives, including patience. Paul actually tells us to clothe ourselves with patience (see Col. 3:12). We need to actively work on growing in each area that these fruits cover, as encouraged by the apostle Paul (see Phil. 1:11).

When do we know that we have mastered patience? When I was crying out to the Lord to send me all those years ago, longing to go right away, what was God's reaction? Did He say, "Now, stop saying 'send me', Claudia." No. I can see the Father's face full of excitement, of joy, because I was moving things in the unseen realms with my prayers and intercession and passion to do what God had called me to do.

And I was also cementing in my whole being—body, soul, and spirit—the calling God had given me. It was not the times of great longing that were worrisome, but the times that longing faded and other things threatened to drown it out. When we run out of patience, we tend to take things into our own hands. How many young people just want to get married and so they marry the wrong person out of lack of patience!

Abraham ran out of patience because God's promise of a son took so long. His wife was beyond child-bearing age, and he himself was an old man. In the natural, the fulfillment of God's promise was not possible. Abraham forgot that God was the God of the impossible, and took matters into his own hands. So Abraham had Ishmael with his servant woman, Hagar; this son became the father of the Muslim faith. Yet, God redeemed Abraham's impatience and gave him the promised son, Isaac, anyway. But Abraham had to live with the consequences of his impatience, and so has every generation since then.

The same is true for Moses. He grew up in the Pharaoh's household, yet knew he was Hebrew. He knew that God had spared his life for a purpose. He knew Abraham's promise from God, "…Know for certain that for four hundred years your descendants will be strangers in a country not their own and that they will be enslaved and mistreated there" (Gen. 15:13).

Moses knew that the end of those 400 years was approaching. He knew it was no coincidence that God had put him into Pharaoh's household and was aware that he had been chosen as His people's deliverer.

Moses was eager to step into his destiny, and his impatience cost him 40 years in the desert, and God's plans were delayed for an additional 30 years. Moses, 390 years after the children of Israel had arrived in Egypt, intervened in a fight to save his Hebrew brother, and killed an Egyptian in the process (see Exod. 2). Moses fled for his life, and had 40 years in the desert to mourn his impatience and learn patience. The second time he wanted to be absolutely sure it was the right time, and that time his hesitation was very great to try again. Because of his impatience, "the length of time the Israelite people lived in Egypt was 430 years" (Exod. 12:40). The first time, he was an overeager deliverer and messed up. The second time, he was a reluctant deliverer and knew that only God could do it through him.

Fallible People

Thank God that He works with fallible people, with those who make mistakes, and still accomplish what He had planned before the foundation of the world. When I felt that pull to go to Bible school in 1994, just months after I got saved, I checked out several Bible colleges and even picked out one. Now did I quit everything and go? No, I did not. I knew that the right time had not come yet. But I did go in that direction.

Every time God tells me something to do, I will take steps in that way. I do everything I can, but I never let go of His hand to make sure He is still right by me. I will go that way until I feel that gentle tug from His hand that lets me know this is not the right direction for now, even though we will eventually go that way.

I did not go to Bible college in 1994, but had to wait until 2001. I did not go to Mali in 1995 when He called me, but had to wait until 2003. And I am not married yet, though He has spoken it over and over, and I am still waiting patiently. Patience is trusting that He knows what is best for me. It is complete confidence that my life is in God's hands, and that He will lead me in His perfect will for His purposes for me. He is the perfect Father who has His child's best interest in mind. He sees the complete picture from eternity until eternity, that we cannot even start to grasp. As I wait upon the fulfillment of God's promises with patience and trust in Him, He is working in the unseen world setting everything into place. If He just opened our eyes for a moment to what is going on behind the scenes, our impatience would be gone right away.

Our time of waiting is also a time of testing. As the time goes by, God watches to see how serious we are about entering into our destiny. I did not just twiddle my thumbs for ten years waiting to get on that plane to

Mali. No, I learned Malian languages, learned more about the people and culture, and studied the Word of God and many books to have as much as possible to give away once the day would come. I also sought God's face, sought spiritual gifts (see 1 Cor. 14:1), and sought every and any equipping that would be useful.

God watches you. He watches to see how you are getting ready for your destiny, and as you do your part, He does His part in preparing you. The more you bring to the table, the earlier you will be ready to launch. And the higher your calling, the longer and deeper the preparation process goes. As time passes, you need to persevere, holding on to His promises, even when everything seems to go the opposite direction and life does not make sense any more. He is still right there with you. He is still accomplishing His purposes. "You need to persevere so that when you have done the will of God, you will receive what He has promised" (Heb. 10:36).

We are in a marathon, not a sprint, and the marathon runner needs to keep going even when the going gets tough if he or she wants to reach the destination (see Heb. 12:1). Learning perseverance is crucial if we want to reach maturity (see James 1:4). "Blessed is the one who perseveres under trial" (James 1:12).

Do you want to be blessed? Can you go on toward your destiny even when everything around you is dark and you have no understanding of what's going on? Did you not ask God to prepare you for your destiny? Did you not ask Him to get you ready, whatever it takes? Could it be that He is answering your prayer and "killing" you?

Dying to Self

Two people want to kill us—satan and God—and I would rather have God kill me. Jesus said, "…unless a kernel of wheat falls to the ground and dies, it remains only a single seed. But if it dies, it produces many seeds" (John 12:24). If you have asked to be a world changer, to become fruitful producing fruit a hundred times over, then there is no way around the process of dying. Jesus said that we must deny ourselves and take up our individual crosses (see Matt. 16:24, Mark 8:34, Luke

9:23). He even stated that we cannot be His disciple if we are not willing to do so (see Luke 14:27).

We all love the first part of Philippians 3:10, "I want to know Christ—yes, to know the power of His resurrection," and quote it all the time. But when have you last finished reading the verse? "...And participation in His sufferings, becoming like Him in His death." Death. What? Do you still love this verse and pray it? Can you truly join in with Paul when he says, "We always carry around in our body the death of Jesus.... For we who are alive are always being given over to death for Jesus' sake.... So then, death is at work in us" (2 Cor. 4:10-12a). Paul urges us (a strong word) "to offer your bodies as living sacrifices, holy and pleasing to God—this is your spiritual act of worship" (Rom. 12:1).

In the old covenant, the Israelites had to bring sacrifices to God. In the new covenant that Jesus made with us, He has taken care of all the sacrifices once and for all. Today, we are the sacrifices on the altar.

Are you offering yourself to Him on the altar of sacrifice? Do you look into His eyes of love and trust Him completely, willingly walking up the steps to the altar that represents death? Fix your eyes on Him and not the knife in His hands. Isaac was about 13 years of age when he found out that his own father was going to sacrifice him to God. Surely he could have overpowered his old father, but he chose to trust this man who had always had his best interest in mind and allowed him to tie him up and put him on his deathbed. If Isaac was willing to do this under the old covenant, how much more should we be willing to lay down our lives and lie down on the cold, stone altar of sacrifice. We can only do it when we have His Holy Spirit living in us, and trust our heavenly Father that the outcome will be good.

When the potter takes a broken vessel that is not good for anything any more, how can he make it beautiful and useful again? He lovingly breaks off the pieces that are out of place, crushes the remaining pieces (see Matt. 21:44), and puts the remains on his potter's wheel. Then he adds life-giving water; water that makes the hard clay soft again and with so much excitement and anticipation of the end-product, he gently starts forming the clay. And suddenly the clump of hard clay starts to take form, starts to look more and more like the vessel with a specific purpose it is meant to be.

Is it fun to be pruned (see John 15:2)? No. Does it hurt for "stuff" to be cut off, removed, and taken away? Yes. But, "If Jesus Christ be God and died for me then no sacrifice can be too great for me to make for Him." This was C.T. Studd's motto, and I adopted it shortly after giving my life to Jesus, striving to live accordingly in every area of my life. Jesus died an unimaginably cruel death on the cross. How can I not give myself to Him completely in return? My self is the only thing I have to offer up to Him, and so I will lie down on His altar.

If this has been bad news for you, I have more bad news: dying is a repeated process that we have to go through over and over again while alive on earth. I cannot count any more how many deaths I have died since the summer of 1993; but every time, I'm surprised again that there was still something else that had to die—sometimes, the same area had sprung back to life again. One of my Bible school professors used to say, "If you are still whining and complaining, you are not dead yet. Dead people don't talk." The more you embrace your death, the faster it will be over with—at least until the next time. Complaining only prolongs the process, as the Israelites had to learn the hard way while wandering in the desert around the same mountain seemingly forever.

News From Vienna

In the summer of 1994, I started writing regular newsletters to keep my friends up to date with what's going on in my life. In the very first one (*News from Vienna 1* available on my Website), I share this story. I had returned from a wonderful trip to England where I had taken 90 unforgettable pictures. However, my bag arrived with a hole and the films were gone. This is what I write, "At first I was terribly sad thinking of all the great souvenirs immortalized on those photos and lost. I couldn't accept it and thought, why did I put the films in this pocket! …Then I remembered that I have *everything* in Jesus and I wondered about the importance these films had for me. So I let them go, I could live without those photos!" I was encouraged to call the airport, and it was a miracle that the films were found and returned to me.

Our God is a jealous God, and He does not accept any other lovers in our lives (see for example Exod. 20:5). Jesus emphasized the most important commandment of all, "Love the Lord your God with all your heart and with all your soul and with all your mind and with all your strength" (Mark 12:30). We are to love Him only. He is to be number one in our lives, and He will not share this place with anyone or anything else. His words to us are even shocking when He says, "Anyone who loves his father or mother more than Me is not worthy of Me; anyone who loves his son or daughter more than Me is not worthy of Me" (Matt. 10:37). Can we truly say that we do not love our family more than Jesus? Can we truly say that we do not love our husband or wife more than Jesus? If we had to choose, who would we choose? What about your car? Do you love your car more than Jesus? Or do you worship your television set, spending more time watching it than hanging out with the Lover of your soul? If you had to give up everything, what would be hardest to let go?

I learned my lesson that Jesus is everything I need that summer of 1994—but it was only the first layer of the onion. In 1996, another layer was taken care of. My laptop computer died. I panicked as there was so much valuable data on it, including my personal journal and university notes. But then I stopped myself and thought, *Don't be stupid. It's only a notebook. Of course, it would be terrible to lose all the data, but you have all you need, you have JESUS.* I was ashamed of having loved my notebook so much and repented of having given it too much importance, telling Jesus that I only wanted and needed Him (quote from *News from Vienna 11*, available on my Website). It was possible to restore the computer and rescue the data.

The next layer was taken care of in 2001. It was just before I left Austria to go to Bible school. At that time, I worked my dream job at IBM in Vienna, a four-month job testing speech recognition software in five different languages. By that time, the Internet had become commonplace, and I also had my laptop computer that had become indispensable to me. I used it for everything imaginable and spent most of my time at home working on it. One day, it simply would not start up. The one-year warranty had just expired, and the motherboard had died. The computer was gone, the data was gone, and I had to spend money I needed to go to the U.S. on a new computer. I was devastated. God was gracious, though, and an IBM colleague was at least able to save my data. I had failed to learn my lesson that time around.

One year later God gave me another chance. By that time, I had already spent one year in Kansas City, and my life had been transformed. One night I returned home from the wonderful service at church to find the police at the house. It had been broken into, and all the computers had been stolen, including mine. As a poor Bible student, it had been the only valuable thing I possessed. Now it was gone, as were my school files, emails, and all the documents that had accumulated over the years. I was shocked. While I was at church worshiping God, He had allowed a thief to violate our property and steal our stuff. I had nothing left on this earth.

Shaken, I spent the night at the house of one of my professors. And that is where I came to the realization that with everything gone, Jesus was all I had left. And then I made a decision and proclaimed it to the heavenlies: *Jesus is enough; Jesus is all I need.* Heaven rejoiced at my response, and the floodgates opened to pour down heavenly blessings. I was filled to overflowing with joy, as nothing on this earth had any claim on me any more. I entered into personal revival that lasted for three weeks, spending countless precious hours in His presence, being filled with His joy over and over again. What the enemy had meant for harm and destruction, God used to bring about a great victory.

No Other Lover

We cannot afford being attached to the things of this world, whether computers, Internet, cars, television, clothes, or whatever else has a prominent place in our lives. Jesus told us, "Do not store up for yourselves treasures on earth, where moths and vermin destroy, and where thieves break in and steal" (Matt. 6:19). Why is it so hard to obey these words? Why are we never content with what we have? Do you really need a new phone, bigger television, newer car? Jesus also said, "where your treasure is, there your heart will be also" (Matt. 6:21). Where do you invest your money? Do you invest it into the latest gadgets, or do you store up treasures in Heaven (v. 20) where they can bring eternal fruit? How would you react if this "stuff" was taken away from you? Your reaction would definitely show where your heart is and who your lover is. What or who you spend most of your time with is who you love most. And I was guilty that it was not Jesus who occupied that place in my life.

As with most everyone in the Western world, I grew up with a television set. It is so easy for a mother to put her kids in front of the television and know they are occupied instead of worrying about what they might be up to. As a single mom, my mother definitely made good use of the free babysitter television set.

When the years of darkness and despair started when I was 12 years of age and Mom's boyfriend moved in, I fled into the fantasy world of television. I would come home from school at 2 P.M., and I was the first at home. Television became my family, especially one soap opera that was on every afternoon. I spent hours in front of the television, able to forget the harsh reality of real life. Television had become the love of my life, my way of coping, as I had no idea at that time that there was a God out there who loved me and who I could have a relationship with. I believe that God gives us ways to cope with life that enable us to make it through the hard times. However, watching television had become a stronghold in my life and had to be dealt with once I became a child of the Kingdom of light.

Baggage

When we start our lives with Jesus, we come with a lot of baggage. We are uncut diamonds with lots of impurities, and our loving, heavenly Father takes His time to gently remove one after the other and grind us into beautiful, precious stones. He knows how much we can take at a time and is in no hurry to make us perfect from one day to another. In fact, brace yourself for this news: It will take all your life. In our microwave, instant culture, we want everything immediately, but we would not even be able to cope with being changed that much from one day to another. And so He starts with one impurity, points it out to us, and helps us as we wrestle to get rid of it.

Shortly after I came to know the Lord, I moved to Paris for half a year where I rented a little room with no access to television. Upon my return to Austria, I moved back in with my family, which was extremely hard as they were so much against my faith. The difficult situation with my mother's boyfriend was ongoing, though it was better than it had been during my teenage years. Still, there were times I had to flee the house and find refuge with friends. All I wanted was to move out and find a place on my own so I could praise and worship God as much as I liked, and would not have to concentrate on being defensive all the time.

I moved into my friend's apartment in 1994 because she was abroad, and was greatly blessed by having a place of my own. However, I moved out a few months later when I realized it was not OK legally for me to be there. I trusted that God would honor my desire to live in total obedience to Him. I had to wait a whole year, living again in my mother's household, before I moved into my own apartment. It was central, cheap, and had neither heating (Austria is cold!), nor running water—therefore no bathroom or shower. There was a toilet outside in the corridor that the five apartments on that floor shared. All I thought was, *Finally a place of my own—and a great way to practice living in Africa.*

In 1998 I finally bought a television to keep me company in the silent apartment. I was very active doing lots of things, taking more classes than average at university, being very involved with the Christian student group and at church, evangelizing friends, and doing so many activities that I am amazed today at how I did it all. But every time I came home, I turned on the television. I guess since I was single it at least filled the apartment with noise.

But God had heard my repeated cries to *Sanctify me, cleanse me, purify me, and make me holy as You are holy*, and He was at work in my life healing me and making me more and more into a reflection of Jesus. He had never told me to or sanctioned my buying the television; and in the fall of 1997, He addressed the issue and asked me clearly to give it up. I immediately objected. "But, Lord, I need to be informed about what's going on in the world, and You often use those reports to break my heart and call me to intercession. I surely can't give it up" (quote from *News from Vienna 18*).

We need to learn not to question God when He tells us to do some-thing. We need to learn to simply obey, whether we understand His rea-son for telling us to do a certain thing or not. Yes, there was truth in my objection, but it did not matter at all. Every day I argued with God, though deep in my heart I knew that I was spending time with the tel-evision instead of Jesus when given the choice, and it did bother me. However, I did not want to give it up, and my continued disobedience started to take a toll. My old self came more and more to the surface as I lived according to my old nature.

The Lord reminded me of my daily prayer. "Lord, I'm ready to pay any price—just use me in the coming revival." And His soft voice replied, "Didn't you say you were willing to pay any price?" I admitted it and knew I had to obey. I was concerned I could miss God's purposes for my life if I continued in my disobedience. The weeks went by, and I got very exhausted even physically. I felt as if I had been running from God for weeks. Christmas was at the door, and one Sunday at church the Lord whispered into my ear, "Give me the television as a birthday present." And I did. My life turned around immediately, with the old nature disappearing where it belonged.

Less than a year later, I got the television back during a time of per-sonal crisis when I felt abandoned by God; but in the beginning of 1999, I gave it up again, giving the antennae into the custody of a friend.

In the summer of 1999 I returned from five months in Mali where I had worked very hard on gathering linguistic data for my thesis. I was physically worn out, and emotionally tired as I had to deal with problems caused by the people who had used my car and lived in my apartment. I did not have the energy to let everyone know I was back, and ended up home alone with nothing to do and the weight of the world on my shoul-ders. I longed to escape reality by watching television, and felt its pull again. A month after my return I had cable TV installed in direct rebellion to God's will for me. Needless to say, things got much worse after that.

Ten months of spiritual darkness, separation from God's presence and God's blessings followed. But God hadn't left me. When I came to church, my heart was aching for His presence…. I was still interpreting the Sunday night services into German (when I was there) and keeping up the Tutoring Club (helping kids with problems in school). There were a few little things during those months that God sent me to show me He was still there (quote from *News from Vienna 24*).

My old nature took control of me again, and I was walking in the flesh. I hated the way I acted, and hardly recognized myself. I was shocked that going to church was suddenly a struggle instead of a joy, and that nobody at all seem to care about where I found myself. There was one lady who was an exception and the only light in my darkness. I had no fellowship with Christians, and felt that I had lost all three that remained—love, faith, and hope. I felt as an embarrassment to God and Christianity and did not want to be with unbelievers.

Just before my birthday in May, I made myself go to one of the international cell-groups of my church where I had attended a few times. That night, God spoke to me throughout the whole evening, through everything that was being said. I heard God's serious voice asking me to make a final decision who I would serve, saying that I could not waiver between the two ways for much longer. That scared me.

At the end of the night, I surrendered the television to God. I knew I needed to act on this decision right away and told the cell-group leaders all about it. Days later I moved into the neighboring apartment where there was a sink—after five years of having no water inside the apartment—and did not have cable installed again. God's sweet presence immediately returned into my life, and all I could do was weep at His goodness. Not only that, all the gifts I felt I had lost during that time were returned and seemed to even be more refined and powerful than ever.

I was overcome by His mercy and grace and broke down weeping. I did not deserve being used by God like this again. All the while, my heavenly Father had been beckoning me to return to Him, to give up my rebellion and obedience and return to His flock. He had been longing to hold me in His arms again and shower His blessings down on me, yet I was not willing. I chose the fleeting comfort of the world to the life-giving comfort of my Maker. I was ignorant of His out-stretched arms, of the tears in His eyes, and the longing in His voice as He whispered for me to come. Yet I turned on the television, placing an object made by man in the position where He belonged to be. Those ten months were the darkest of my Christian life, and I would not have believed anyone had they told me that I would act that way. I was shocked and learned the lesson of how dangerous willful dis-obedience is, and that any of us can fall deeply.

Did any part of my story resound within you? Do you spend more time with your lover television than your Lover, Jesus? Then repent right now, and place Jesus first in your life again, and His presence and blessings will return.

Letting Go

Sometimes the things we hold on to are more subtle and don't seem to really make a difference in our lives. Before I came to know the Lord, my life centered on two passions—dancing and astronomy. Since I moved to Paris shortly after my conversion, I automatically stopped dancing and simply did not take it up again. It hurt to be stripped of what I loved, but years later God redeemed my passion for dancing.

Returning from Paris, I knew I could not finish my astronomy and physics studies, and God had already told me that he was sending me to French-speaking Africa as a missionary. I was lacking just one credit hour to a Bachelor's degree and tried several times to do that one credit hour in computing. However, I was unable to complete it.

During my ten months in Canada in 1996, the Lord spoke to me to give up astronomy. I was still holding on to this remnant of my old life, wanting at least that degree to have something to show for all the hard work I had put in. In the third chapter of his letter to the Philippians Paul gives an impressive list of all that he had going for him. Yet, he con-tinues to say that "whatever were gains to me I now consider loss for the sake of Christ. ...I consider them garbage" (Phil. 3:7-8b). What strong words used by Paul! I was holding on to my past, holding on to my accomplishments, but God wanted me to release them to Him and walk on free into His purposes for me.

Yes, I can list academic accomplishments—Bachelor's degree in physics, and nearly one in astronomy, Master's degree in African languages and French, Master's of Divinity and Doctorate of theology. I spent 12 years of my life going to school, and another 12 years going to university/college. Was it worth it? Most definitely. I enjoyed (almost) every minute of it. Does it count anything in the eyes of God? Not in and of itself. God does not look at our worldly accomplishments; He looks at our hearts. He wants us to surrender every treasure we have on earth to Him, including our degrees and careers.

Maybe it is your job, your career, that has taken the first place in your life banning Jesus to second place. Are you able to surrender it to Him? Are you willing to lay your career on the altar for His scrutiny? Will you seek His Kingdom first, and let Him take care of the rest?

Testings

The moment you say yes, your commitment will be tested. When I finished my studies in Vienna in December 2000, I asked the Lord whether to go to Bible school as I had always dreamed of doing or go straight to Mali. The time for me to step into my destiny was closer than ever. Yet, there was still half a year until the beginning of the next term, and I had lots of debts that I told God I would not leave Austria with. In January 2001, I accepted my dream job, combining my love for languages and computers. For four months I worked that 40-hour job with passion and integrity, and the project was completed just days before I left Austria to move to Kansas City. A few weeks before leaving, my boss offered me a new and better contract, trying to get me to stay at IBM. From the world's perspective, it was very tempting. But I know what God had spoken to me, and I know that my time in Austria was over. I turned down that lucrative contract, and never regretted it.

After getting another Master's degree and a doctorate in Kansas City in 2003, I went to Mali. Did any of the street children ever ask me about my credentials? No. Did anyone truly care? No. What they cared about was that I loved them and was there to serve them, counting my academic accomplishments all loss for the sake of knowing God and making Him known. Jesus was, and is, number one in my life, above everything else. Over and over I had died in the course of the years so the old nature and desires of this world had nothing to hold on to in my life.

Holiness

From the very beginning, I had a very strong desire to be holy, to be clean before God and get rid of all sin in my life. The writer of Hebrews exhorts us to "throw off everything that hinders and the sin that so easily entangles. And let us run with perseverance the race marked out for us" (Heb. 12:1b). We cannot hold televisions, cars, or phones in our hands while running this race. We cannot have sin wound around us, tripping us up, and slowing us down or even making us veer off the race track. We need to read His Word and check whether we live up to the standards in it.

The Word is compared to a mirror that shows us what we look like (see 1 Cor. 13:12, James 1:23). We cannot put dark sunglasses on so we won't see the ugly face looking back at us. And we cannot afford to stay in denial and think everything looks just wonderful. No, we must look more closely. We must join in with David who prayed, "Search me, God, and know my heart; test me and know my anxious thoughts. See if there is any offensive way in me..." (Ps. 139:23-24). That was a bold prayer, and we need to brace ourselves for when God responds to this prayer, because we won't like it. We will be shocked by what is hidden in our hearts. It's ugly, but it is necessary so we can rid ourselves of all sin, of everything that is not pleasing to the Lord.

You may wonder, *What is the point? Why should I care? Let what is hidden stay hidden. I'm happy with the way my life is right now.* It is so easy and much more comfortable to stay standing where you are and enjoy the countryside. But standing means not moving on. Do you want to reach the goal? Do you want to enter into your destiny? Then there is no way around sanctification and holiness. God said, "Be holy as I am holy"

(Lev 11:44, 1 Pet. 1:16). Peter said, "Be holy in all you do" (1 Pet. 1:15), not just when it is easy and does not require effort. Surely it is possible if God gave us this command, and if we want to please our Lord, Savior, and Lover, then we need to obey His words. And it is so worth it!

Besides His pleasure and joy, Jesus also said, "Blessed are the pure in heart for they will see God" (Matt. 5:8). Wow, what a wonderful promise! And He is not just talking about eternity with Him, but the here and now. Our God is a holy God, and only that which is holy can enter into His presence. Jesus paid the ultimate price so we would be cleansed of our sin. The way is open for us to approach the throne of God boldly (see Heb. 4:16). "Who may ascend the mountain of the Lord? Who may stand in His holy place? The one who has clean hands and a pure heart..." (Ps. 24:3-4a). While Jesus has done it once and for all, we do need to come to Him to be cleansed over and over again. And the longer we do, the deeper the cleansing goes, reaching deeper and deeper to the yet untouched layers, as He deals with one sin or bad behavior after another.

Sinfulness

David heart's cry was, "Create in me a pure heart, O God, and renew a steadfast spirit within me" (Ps. 51:10), which he prayed right after he had had a taste of what was in the hidden corner of his heart, not only committing adultery but even murder. The same way we are all capable of great things for God, we are all capable of the most horrible things we do not think we are capable of. Let no one think he or she is immune to sin. That is pride and will certainly lead to downfall, just as I thought I would never walk away from God and yet persisted in rebellion doing just that for ten months.

From the very beginning, I had an acute awareness of the sin and brokenness in my life. Even the week I got saved I knew I had to reconcile with my friend before being able to come to the Lord. Without anyone telling me, I knew that I could no longer cheat or lie, which had a serious affect on my studies. I never again cheated during tests and exams. I rested in the arms of my God. I was no longer nervous, but had total peace when I wrote an exam, knowing I had done everything possible, and God would help me. And my grades were better than ever.

When I came to the Lord, I had a court case looming over me because of somebody else's lack of integrity, but it was my name on the contract that had been broken, and I had signed it while still 17 years old. Mom and my lawyer pressured me to lie to the judge so I would not be held accountable, but I refused. Mom was stunned by my peace in the midst of it all. In the end, I had to pay a large amount of money as a fine, which was not easy. In the world's eyes, that was stupid.

But it was not the only stupid thing I did that earned me the adjective "crazy" by my family. I have already told you about the apartment I gave up at great cost because I could not stay there legally, though nobody would have known. I was also earning money by teaching my private students, and that money was not taxed. While everybody does that in Austria, when I found out that it was in reality illegal, I took the right steps to obey the laws of my country. While I paid a very high price financially (taxes in Austria are half the salary), it was worth it as I declared every hour I taught and paid taxes on all my income.

When I moved to Kansas City in 2001, I was a student and therefore not allowed to work. I obeyed the law, learning to trust my heavenly Father to take care of me, though it was not easy paying tuition and living in the U.S. without working for two years.

There were seasons when my longing to be pure and holy increased, and God heard my heart's cry. I remember a special season in the beginning of 1996 when God showed me several things I had to make right because it was sin in my life. I was guilty of the sin of stealing. I had property in my possession that was not mine. My mom had stored her teenage diaries in my room, and I had kept them. I returned them to her. I had teaching books I had borrowed from one of my student teachers five years earlier that I had never returned. It was a challenge, but I found the school, wrote a letter of apology to the teacher, and gave them back. I still had a box of Commodore 64 floppy discs my friend's boyfriend had lent me years earlier. I searched for him, found him, and called him. He was surprised and told me to throw them away. I had pictures that belonged to my primary school teacher that I returned, as well as pictures belonging to my mom. Everything that was not mine was returned to their rightful owners.

God was so pleased with my actions that I could feel His face smiling upon me, and He greatly blessed me at a conference shortly afterward.

Do you want to see the Lord's favor on your life? Do you still have anything in your possession that is not yours? Are you willing to return these items to their owners, even if it possibly means dire consequences?

I threw away much after starting my life with Jesus. I love books, and I had had a keen interest in esotericism for a while, with a friend of mine who was deeply involved in the occult. Thankfully the Lord protected me from ever joining in with his rituals. However, there were many books to be thrown and destroyed. I was an expert in ufology and had even considered working in that field after finishing my astronomy studies. I believe that UFOs are definitely real; but after I knew the Lord, I understood that it is simply demonic. All those books had to go to. And then I still had my beloved Stephen King books; books that go under your skin. I decided to burn them.

Besides returning stuff to their owners or to the trash, I also had to learn to let go of things. Jesus said, "Give to everyone who asks you, and if anyone takes what belongs to you, do not demand it back" (Luke 6:30). That is a challenging verse. When I returned from my first U.S. trip in 1997 (the 10-week school in 1996 was in Canada), I brought back an awesome video from a well-known church in Toronto, and I could hardly wait to watch it. An African brother saw it and wanted to borrow it for just a week; I really wanted to watch it myself, but gave in and let him have it. The following Sunday, he did not have it with him, and neither the following, or the following, or the following. I got angry because I wanted *my* video back. Then the Lord gently reminded me that it was *His* video, as is everything else He has entrusted to my care. I surrendered the video to God. I forgot all about it until one year later, when this brother returned the video to me. Sometimes, when we surrender items to God, He returns them to us when He sees fit.

~

Precious Jesus, thank You for loving me. I confess that I have put other people and things ahead of You in my life, and I ask Your forgiveness. I offer myself as a living sacrifice today and give You permission to do a deep work of cleansing and killing me. Thank You for making me into a beautiful vessel that has the honor of carrying Your glory, power, and presence.

Change Points

1. As you are transformed into God's image more and more, the fruit of the spirit grows in your life, including patience.

2. God starts with one impurity, points it out to you, and helps you wrestle to get rid of it.

3. God does not look at your worldly accomplishments; He looks at your heart.

4. While Jesus has done it once and for all, you do need to come to Him to be cleansed over and over again.

5. Do you want to see the Lord's favor on your life?

Chapter Six

Money Issues and Humility

Money Issues and Humility

I had many lessons to learn in the financial arena, and every one prepared me to be able to go to Mali with no money or possessions. The place I had to start from was not an easy one. While my family was never poor, with my high society grandfather helping my mom, it seemed that a financial curse had been on us for generations. My biological father had been struggling all his life, and my mom had a hard time as well. I was still a young teenager when my mom decided to give me all the child support money my father sent her monthly in return for paying a contribution for rent, utilities, and food. I was doing well at the time, but as the years passed, even after becoming a Christian, my financial situation got continually worse. While I was attending the university, my father lost his job, and soon after stopped sending money. I had no source of income left but what I earned through teaching.

As a new believer, it did not take long for me to hear about the principle of tithing—giving a tenth of all we have to the Lord. It is a principle of the old covenant that Jesus encouraged, though even back then the Israelites really did give much more to God in total. Certainly, today He does not want us to follow the Law, but He wants us to give ourselves totally to Him, all we have and possess, all we are. In that respect, 10 percent of all we earn really is not that much to give to Him at all.

I have always loved giving, and so I gave my 10 percent to God with joy. I discovered the truth of Jesus' words that "it is more blessed to give than to receive" (Acts 20:35). I read a few books on the subject, and because of different teachings, found myself in the dilemma of whether the 10 percent needed to go to my local church or not. So I simply started to give 20 percent—10 percent to my church, and 10 percent to ministries and individuals in need—and I have not stopped since. I was passionate about giving, especially giving anonymously. I remember when I once put money on a girl's bed who was very much in need. She was in tears and never found out it had come from me. Even today I keep back beautiful new coins in Mali and sometimes hide them in my kids' stuff for them to find.

Sowing and Reaping

I learned the principle of sowing and reaping. Jesus said, "Give, and it will be given to you. A good measure, pressed down, shaken together and running over, will be poured into your lap. For with the measure you use, it will be measured to you" (Luke 6:38). While this applies to everything, it definitely applies to giving as well. And I was going to prove it, trying to out-give God, and always striving to raise my giving level. But that generational curse was holding me back. Every time I was getting better financially, something would happen to bring me back to zero. There were many desperate moments when I had no money and did not know what to do; but God always took care of me in the last moment. Sometimes money arrived and I didn't have a clue where it came from; other times I found food on my doorstep. My heavenly Father takes care of His children.

I have countless stories that show God's faithfulness and the great interest rate of His heavenly bank. One time in 1996, I anonymously gave $30 to a missionary couple in Vienna. A few weeks later, they put $50 into my hand. Another time I needed $1,600 right away. I only had $200 and thought of a principle I had heard, "If what you have is not enough to meet your need, then it's seed." So I sowed the money, having nothing left, and received the full $1,600 a few days later.

In spite of continual giving, I was not recovering financially. I had opened my first bank account at the age of 15, and it had been overdrawn for most of the time (the way to make debts in the banking system in Austria), especially after becoming a Christian. The struggles were tough and tiring, but I never lost my joy of giving to the needy and to the Lord.

When I finished my studies in December 2000, I was so much in debt that I could literally not make any more debt. After the summer holiday, none of my private students had returned, none of the language schools needed me, and nothing else worked out to earn any money. While not working allowed me to focus totally on finishing my Master's thesis and preparing for my final big exam, my bank account approached more and more my overdraft limit until it was reached. I knew God had called me to go to Bible school the following fall, but there was still this money issue. So I told God that I would not leave Austria while in debt. If He wanted me to go to Bible school in Kansas City, He needed to enable me to pay back my debts and leave Austria with no baggage. The Lord took me at my word, and I was blown away when He took this insurmountable mountain and simply removed it.

In January, I got my dream job testing speech-recognition software at IBM; a project that ended just when I had to leave Austria. Then my private students came back. Then the language schools came back, and I agreed to a few evening classes. And finally a company gave me a 180-page manual to translate into English. For months I worked at IBM all day, then headed to my private students or language school, only to come home at 10 P.M. to work on the translation. This went on for a few months, and by the end of May my body was totally worn out. Days before flying to the U.S., I had a breakdown on the street. Once I was in the U.S., I had these attacks a few more times and was worried, wondering what they were until I found out that they were migraine headache attacks. I had never had a migraine in my life, and have never had one since. I believe they were the price to pay for non-stop working for months.

But by the end of May all my debts were gone and I had a little money to make it through the first two months of my linguistic courses at summer school in Grand Forks, North Dakota. God had done the impossible.

The financial difficulties continued in America, but I held on to God's promise that He would take care of me, even though I was not allowed to work. The first few months I had an apartment in Kansas City, but I struggled greatly in paying my bills and buying food, as well as paying my tuition. I remember when I sent a check for my rent in December, having faith that the money would be in the account by the time the recipient would cash the check two days later. But I was disappointed and had to pay a fee to the bank for going below zero. The cycle of financial setback whenever I was doing better continued, and in the beginning of 2002 I had enough.

Breaking the Curse

One day, one of my Bible school professors and all the students surrounded me and broke off that curse on my life. I could feel God's power answering their prayer. It was the turning point. The curse was truly broken, as time showed. I was in a very desperate situation at that time, and had been having problems with the person in Austria who had moved into my apartment. I had to give up the apartment, but did not know how to get rid of my furniture as I could only return the apartment empty. So at the time of my greatest need when I did not know how to eat or pay tuition, I gave away everything I had left in Austria.

I will never forget the letter I received from a German missionary who had just moved to Austria, and into an empty apartment not knowing how to furnish it. Tears ran down my cheeks as she thanked me for giving away my furniture when she did not have any money to furnish her apartment. At that moment my need was not important any more. I was greatly blessed to know that my sacrifice had brought so much blessing into somebody else's life.

I was on the road to discovery, and no more big financial disasters came to take away all I had. When my computer was stolen in 2002, the insurance company gave me so much money for it that I was able to buy an even nicer computer, plus I had just made a backup of my files and therefore lost very little data.

In the fall of 2002, I had an awesome encounter with the Lord when He showed me a vision. I was kneeling on the ground wearing a stunning golden garment that I marveled at. Then I put my hands into the pockets, and felt some things inside; when I pulled my hands out of the pockets, they were filled with beautiful, shiny, gold coins. Again I marveled. Then Jesus said to me, "As long as you keep giving them away, these pockets will never go empty." I put my hands in, pulled out coins, put them in again, and pulled out more coins, and there was always more. I had been in a season of much sowing, and had just given away my last money, so that vision was an enormous encouragement in light of my great financial need. The Lord has stayed true to His promise. Oh how I love giving it away, blessing God's children!

God Provides

In 2003, I needed $3,000 to go on a missions trip to Malawi and South Africa; an amount that was so big I knew I would watch God in awe provide it. Early in the beginning of 2002, God had spoken to me very clearly that there were two things I needed to do before going to Mali for good. One thing was to go on a missions trip with a well-known evangelist, and the other to visit a well-known missionary in Africa. I was amazed when I found out that those two were going to work together in June 2003, just after I finished school. I knew that was what God had meant for me. However, the deadline for the payment approached, and all I had was $200. So I decided to sow that money, and send it ahead to Africa to Heidi's ministry. When it seemed that the deadline would come and go, I asked the Lord again to make sure He wanted me to go on that trip, and He replied in the affirmative. That's all I needed to hear. It was not my responsibility to worry about the money. When God calls, He provides. I have always lived according to this principle.

Just before the deadline, I was at church Sunday morning and received prayer for finances. When I walked away from the front of the church, a lady approached me and told me God had spoken to her and her husband independently to pay for the whole missions trip. My knees nearly buckled right there and then! As expected, I was totally in awe and overwhelmed by the goodness of God.

I walked to the car my friends allowed me to use and started to drive to a friend's wedding. It was raining, and the street was wet. As I turned the corner, my car suddenly continued turning and spinning and hit the side of the road until it came to a complete stop in the middle of the road. I was in shock and just sat there watching church members drive by. Miraculously I was not injured, but the car was totally wrecked. I felt bad about it, but was happy when I heard my friends got more money for it than they had paid for it. For me, it was not a coincidence that the accident happened just after my important trip to Africa had become possible. The enemy knew that after this trip the way was open for me to go to Mali, and he tried one more time to keep that from happening.

In August I was back in Kansas City to pack, attend graduation, say good-bye, and get ready to move to Mali. I had no money, and no idea how I would finance shipping my few belongings over there, or even buying a ticket. However, I reminded myself those were God's problems not mine. Since He was so clearly sending me, He would provide.

Just before I left, my mentor and spiritual mom Jill Austin held a conference, and my new friend Debbie was teaching one of the seminars. I decided to attend her seminar to support her, not knowing that God was up to a sovereign act to encourage me. At the end of her seminar, she asked me forward to pray for me, telling people I was moving to Africa. Suddenly a young girl came forward and put a check with a map of Africa on it at my feet. And then one person after another came and did the same, even giving to the girl who had given her last money. I was blown away and understood my Father's message. *I am your Provider, I am sending you, I will take care of you as I have always done.*

A month later I was on the plane to Mali with no money, no supporters, no mission agency—just a few intercessors, and a big God who owns everything in the universe and was going to take care of me. There were many desperate moments when I cried out to Him for provision and wondered why His people did not help; but in the end, every one of those situations turned into testimonies of praise because of the great faithfulness of our God.

Seek First His Kingdom

If all you give God is your money—whether 10, 20, 50, or even 100 percent—you are in sin, even if you have allowed Him to purify you and remove all the sins of commissions. There are also sins of *omission*. God does not just want your possessions, He wants *you*. He wants everything. He wants your time and your heart. He wants you to seek first His Kingdom and trust Him that He will take care of you (see Matt. 6:33), providing for every need you have.

How tragic it is when fathers or mothers seek after money or fame, neglecting the precious children God has given them. How tragic when our only thoughts are on how to get the next new gadget and it never crosses our mind that God has entrusted us with money to be used for His glory. Let us seek Him, let us seek His Kingdom, let us give Him our time.

What if we started tithing our time to Him, the same way we give our money tithe? It is so much easier to just give money which only takes a second. But how much harder is it to give 10 percent of our time to Him, which would be 144 minutes a day. You may be thinking, *Are you kidding me? Nearly two and a half hours? I have too much work to do, I cannot possibly even give a half hour to God each day*. I encourage you to make an honest list of your activities on a typical day—work, meal times, workout, house work, television time, etc.—and then reorder your priorities. *OK, I will watch less television, I can worship God and pray while doing dishes and while running on the treadmill*. Your beloved Jesus wants to be on your mind and heart continually, whether you are working out, working at your desk, or doing the dishes. Every time you're in the bath room, you have a chance to lift your heart and praises to Him and tell Him how wonderful He is. That is giving our all to Him.

From time to time I love thinking about how I can do something special for Jesus, something outrageous to "surprise" Him and bring joy to His heart. The woman with the alabaster jar of oil did just that. She loved Jesus outrageously, and did an outrageous act of pouring very costly perfume on Jesus' head and feet (see Matt. 26, Mark 14, Luke 7). Her act of great love has not gone unnoticed, and has been told from generation to generation for all eternity.

When we love someone, we want to bless that person, do good things for that person. When I came to know the Lord in 1993, I immediately thought of ways to bless my mom and her boyfriend. I gave my mom flowers, and rented a movie for them that they had always wanted to watch. When my friends would mention something they really wanted, I would keep it in mind to get it for them for their birthdays or Christmas. I also blessed each church I was part of by more than just giving money. A few years ago I was visiting from Africa and found out that my beloved church had a great need for people to help with cleaning. I was excited about this opportunity to bless and honor my church! As I cleaned the toilets, I was full of joy and pride that I was able to serve my church, and prayed blessings over them the whole time I was cleaning. What I loved most was that I was able to do it without anyone but the person responsible knowing. How wonderful it is to serve for God's eyes only!

Servanthood

Jesus said that those who want to be great should be the servant of all (see Matt. 20:26-27, Mark 10:43-44). He Himself gave us the greatest example—He left His glory in Heaven and became a finite human being. And He did not come as a king, but as a baby, a carpenter's son, learning to work hard for His daily bread. He did not come to be served but to serve (see Matt. 20:28, Mark 10:45). His whole life was lived as a servant to others, and at the last supper, He even did a slave's job when He washed His disciple's feet. The ultimate selfless act was when He died on the cross for us. If we want to be like Jesus, we have to become servants. We have to humble ourselves and consider others better than ourselves, serving them (Phil. 2:3).

I have had a few great men and women of God in my life who I loved so much that all I wanted was to serve them. I wanted to be there to carry their bag, to hand them a bottle of water, to give them a pen when they needed it, whatever it was I could do. I considered it a great honor to do the smallest things for them. If we act like this with human beings, how much more should we want to serve Jesus with all our hearts and strength? Jesus, what do You need today? What can I do for You today? How can I bless You and bring You joy today?

Humility

God has given us many talents and abilities, and while we can make money with them, it would be tragic not to use them for the Kingdom of God as well. Yes, I was teaching to make money and finance attending university, but I also started the Tutoring Club at church, using my abilities for free to serve God and His Kingdom. In the fall of 1994 I interpreted simultaneously for the first time as there was a visitor at the meeting who did not speak a word of German. I discovered how it easy it was for me and how much joy I got out of it. From then on I jumped on every opportunity I had to interpret. My church installed interpretation booths so that the Sunday night international service could be translated into several languages. Even when I was the most discouraged, my spirit was lifted when I got into that booth and simply repeated the pastor's words—yes, in the other language. I was a natural, even finding my mind wandering at times, with my mouth continuing to interpret. People loved it when I interpreted, and I had a great passion for it.

The day of testing came when the church had a speaker for a few days of special meetings, and I was not the one chosen to interpret from the front of the church. I knew I could do a better job than the other person and was tempted to be offended at being passed over. But I stopped myself, started blessing the other interpreter, and prayed for him as he interpreted. I submitted to the pastor's decision of choosing him, and thanked God for an opportunity to practice humility. I knew that if I continued serving in the hidden place in humility, the Lord was watching and would lift me up in His time.

When we serve Him wholeheartedly with what He has given us, the day will surely come when He entrusts even more to us (see Luke 19:17).

Humility is maybe the most important key for you to step into your destiny, and it may also be the most lacking in our world today. We have brought the ways of Hollywood into the Christian world, putting ministers on pedestals and nearly worshiping them, making it very hard for them to stay humble. Many have not guarded their hearts against pride, but have allowed it to grow. However, "pride goes before destruction, a haughty spirit before the fall" (Prov. 16:18). God hates pride (see Prov. 8:13) and promises that the proud will not go unpunished (Prov. 16:5, Ps. 101:5). He even opposes them (1 Pet. 5:5, James 4:6). Oh what a terrible thing to be opposed by God! What a tragedy when our heavenly Father has to be against His own beloved children. It breaks His heart to see His children think they are big shots, that they have what they have because of their hard labor and work. He has tears in His eyes when we claim all the glory for our accomplishments when in reality, we could not have done the smallest thing without Him. God chooses:

> *the foolish things of the world to shame the wise…the weak things of the world to shame the strong…the lowly things of this world and the despised things and the things that are not…so that no one may boast before Him* (1 Corinthians 1:27-29).

I definitely qualified as foolish, weak, lowly, despised and even non-existent in the eyes of the world. Growing up I often felt totally forgotten, abandoned, unloved, and lonely. I felt like I was invisible to everyone, and a burden to the world. But there was One who did see me. There was One who said, "Her, I can pick her, because she has nothing to offer. Because I can make My name great through her. Everybody will be amazed to see that someone like her could be used to do great exploits for Me, and they will praise My name."

Fear of Pride

Maybe that is why I have such a fear of pride, such a dread of finding anything proud within me. I seek to clothe myself with humility at all times (see 1 Pet. 5:5). I seek to humble myself before the Lord continually (see James 4:10, 1 Pet. 5:6). I strive to consider others better than myself (see Phil. 2:3, Titus 3:2). When I am criticized—even when it is done in the most inappropriate way and seems totally ridiculous—I go before the Lord to find out if there is even just one kernel of truth in it, and get rid of it. When I am praised, I cannot help but direct people's attention to my heavenly Father who deserves all the praise. I cannot accept any of His glory for myself.

All I ever did was give my life to Him, take His hand and walk on this path simply doing what He would tell me. How can I take any credit for that? He is the One who did everything; I was simply the channel, the instrument He chose. I cannot ever put the two words "my ministry" together as that combination of words seems an abomination to me. It's not my ministry, it is Jesus' ministry that I have the honor of leading and doing, and while it might be easier to simply say "my ministry," you will never hear me say it.

Everything I have is His. Everything I do, I do thanks to His grace and power working through me. I get to be His channel. I get to be His vessel. I get to be His hands and feet, eyes, ears and mouth on this earth, and there is nothing more glorious. May I continually check myself for any trace of pride within me.

As we pursue humility, it is easy to fall into the sin of pride. As we seek humility, we can feel good with our progress, and therefore fall back into pride. I remember a season in 1998 when I was working hard on getting rid of pride. I had just had wonderful experiences in the presence of God, where He had done a lot of things, and I was going on a one-week retreat organized by the Christian student group, which was made up of more conservative Christians than I was. I was checking my motives for even attending the retreat, and brought my pride to the cross, humbling myself until the only motivation left was to go there to serve and love these students.

Even though I had tried so hard, I failed miserably. On the last day, I was approached by one of the leaders who told me that a lot of spiritual pride had come across from me all week. I was shattered and my heart totally broken as I came before the Lord and allowed Him to tear even more pride out of my heart. I thanked the Lord for loving me so much that He would point out my sin to me, convict me, and cleanse me.

With my love of learning, studying, and working hard at my studies, it was also very easy for me to fall into pride when it came to my academic accomplishments. I loved studying, especially when I majored in African studies and French. I always worked as unto the Lord, and knew that my great grades were all due to Him, as I surrendered everything to Him and asked Him to glorify Himself through me. In 1998, I had only one French class to finish that part of my studies. I had always been an excellent student in French, and expected a good grade. Instead, I failed the written exam and was in total shock, unable to figure out how that could have happened. I realized that I had become prideful of my good command of the French language, and had trusted more in my own ability than in God. I repented and thanked the Lord for humbling me and exposing my pride. I paid a high price, having to take the whole class again.

I have learned many lessons in humility over the years, and they will never end while on earth. Pride entered the world with Adam's fall, and we must continually rid ourselves of it. Let's fix our eyes on Jesus, the perfect example of humility, and become more like Him every day.

Search your heart right now, and ask Him to show you where there is even the smallest trace of pride anywhere in your heart. Let your heart be broken at the sight of your pride, and repent of it, asking Him to rip it out and cleanse you. Listen, pastor so-and-so, apostle so-and-so, prophet so-and-so, God is not interested in your position and great title. He is interested in your heart. Are you a servant to all? Do you resemble Jesus, the greatest Servant of all? Do you consider others better than yourself?

Integrity

We need to become men and women of integrity. We need to be above reproach (see 1 Tim. 3:2). We must be holy, clean vessels so He can pour His treasure into us "to show that this all-surpassing power is from God and not from us" (2 Cor. 4:7). His beautiful Holy Spirit loves to live in a clean vessel.

God wants to fill us with more and more of His glory, the greatest treasure that exists in the universe, so He can tip us over and pour out His glory, His living waters, to a desperate and dying world around us. So we can shine brightly in a world filled with darkness. So we resemble Jesus and are reflections and images of Him to those who do not know Him. All it takes is for us to get on that altar and let Him operate on us. We need to stay on the Potter's wheel and allow Him to break us to pieces so He can make a new, beautiful vessel out of us. And when we thought we were done, finally we are that complete, whole vessel, then He puts us into the kiln where hot, blazing fire makes us even more beautiful and finishes the process so we can be used for the purpose we were created.

What are the keys in our preparation process to becoming world-changers? We need to surrender everything to our Beloved and put Him first in our lives, having no other lovers beside Him. We need to be free from all attachments to material things, things that pass, things that hold us back, even those things that are good. We need to humble ourselves before Him as well as others and walk in humility, serving others and considering them better than ourselves (see Rom. 11:18).

We need to rid ourselves of all sin, any blemish, anything that is not pleasing to our heavenly Father, and allow Him to sanctify us, purify us, and mold us into the image of Jesus. We need to crucify our flesh and die to ourselves so that nothing but Him remains in us. We need to be people of integrity, beyond any hint of reproach, whether that be in the financial or any other arena. We need to move forward patiently, seeking Him as well as seeking the equipping necessary, and go through the trials and tests God has ordained for us with joyful and grateful hearts even in the times when we do not understand what is going on.

Does this seem like God is asking a lot of us? It might seem overwhelming, but at the hand of our heavenly Father we are able to move forward and will come out of the furnace cleansed, pure, a precious golden vessel to be used for His glory. Are you ready? Then pray with me:

Dear heavenly Father, precious Jesus, thank You for loving me too much to leave me the way I am. I confess that I have put other people and things ahead of You in my life, and I ask Your forgiveness. I choose today to make You number one in my life, and to love You more than anything else in this world. I offer myself as a living sacrifice today and give You permission to do a deep work of cleansing and killing me. Thank You for making me into a beautiful vessel that has the honor of carrying Your glory, power, and presence. I want to be holy, pure, full of integrity and humility, and I cannot achieve it in my own strength.

Thank You that Your power is made perfect in my weakness and that You continue to make me more and more into the image of Jesus. Thank You for Your love and faithfulness that is so much greater than I can even imagine. I trust You and praise You in advance for the amazing vessel You are making me into, so I can step into the awesome destiny You have designed especially for me.

~

Father, I desire to be holy, pure, full of integrity and humility, a son or daughter who is pleasing to You in every way. I choose to live a life of joyful servanthood, of giving of everything I possess, everything I am and everything I do. I thank You that Your power is made perfect in my weakness, and that You continue to transform me into the likeness of Jesus. I praise You in advance for the amazing vessel You are making me into, so I can step into the destiny You have for me and become a world changer for Your eternal Kingdom. Hallelujah!

Change Points

1. God wants you to give yourself totally to Him, all you have and possess, all you are.

2. As long as you keep giving money away to those in need, your pockets will never go empty.

3. Many have not guarded their hearts against pride, but have allowed it to grow.

4. God has given you many talents and abilities, and while you can make money with them, it would be tragic not to use them for the Kingdom of God as well.

5. Search your heart right now, and ask Him to show you where there is even the smallest trace of pride anywhere in your heart.

Chapter Seven

Healing for Your Heart

Healing for Your Heart

By now we know what to do to get ourselves ready for the great destiny God has for us. We know the areas in our lives where we need to reorder our priorities and that we need to work on. We can take proactive steps to grow in each one of the areas, working out our salvation in cooperation with our heavenly Father.

Yeah, you are on track! You are going in the right direction! So are you ready for more? Are you ready to go even deeper? Yes, you have paid a price; you have gone through pain as you die to self, but now it is time to let God enter into the most painful corners of your heart. Allow your gentle, loving, heavenly Father to bring light into the darkest areas of your heart that you have locked away and thrown away the key. Even though you don't have a key any more, He has the master key, and He is just waiting for your permission to put that key into the lock, and walk into the place of horror, the place of unimaginable pain, the place that you do not ever want to be reminded of ever again.

Look into His eyes of love. Look into His eyes of compassion. See your pain reflected in His eyes. He has felt every blow you had to take, every word that cut through your being, every touch that destroyed your soul. Every tear you cried also rolled down His cheek. He knows your pain. And He is the only One with an answer to your pain. He is the only One who gave His life for you so you could be free from your pain, so you could be healed totally—spirit, soul, and body. He did not just watch you suffer, He suffered as well. He did not stay passive, He actively gave His life and suffered the most cruel day, death on a cross. He has acted, He has paid the ultimate price so that you could be set free and healed and live the life in the abundance that He has prepared specially for you.

We have already established that the world is being ruled by God's enemy who is out to destroy what God loves most—humankind. He is doing a good job at influencing people to do the most atrocious, vile, unimaginable acts of hell. I had my own share of sampling those. But God is so much greater than all of that. He is the One who created us, He is the One who gave us life. And He is the One who laid down His life to save us out of the kingdom of darkness and bring us into His Kingdom of life where the enemy has no rights whatsoever. Satan's rule is broken, his reign over our lives is gone; he has no more authority over us. The war was won when Jesus breathed his last on the cross and came back to life three days later.

The Healer

The day we choose to follow Jesus is our victory day. However, even when people are liberated from the domination of the enemy, they do not necessarily look like winners. They are injured, bruised, starved, and in bad shape and need to heal inside and out and learn to live in their new state of freedom. When we accept Jesus' victory for ourselves, we start a new life of freedom, but we do not come without baggage. Years of living as a slave in the kingdom of darkness under a the rule of a cruel dictator has taken its toll on us, and we need to let the great Healer tend to our wounds, clean us up, bind us up, and put on us healing balm.

When you go to the doctor because of an injury or disease, he might hurt you even more as he removes the source of your pain, the piece of glass in your wound, or the pus that is infecting your body. But you know that the pain is temporary, and that the result will be worth it—healing and restoration, no more sickness. You trust your doctor. Now I invite you to trust Your loving, heavenly Father who knows better than anyone else in this universe what is best for you. He does not want you to continue living in misery, in bondage, letting satan still rule in your life though you are not in his kingdom any more. God invites you to get on the operating table so He can start to slowly mend your heart and remove the lies that bind you.

Maybe you feel like you have been very successful in pushing down your pain, in hiding it as deep down as possible, and keeping yourself busy so you do not have time to think of it. Maybe you have achieved a life you are content with. Does that mean you are truly free and healed? No. I assure you that what stays hidden cannot stay hidden forever. It takes so much energy to live like that, and you will eventually break down as a result.

You cannot afford to live in denial any longer. You cannot afford to stop in your walk with God any more. You may have lived with the effects of your painful childhood for years, even decades, and are not an inch closer to living the fullness of life God has promised you. You are still far from living your dream. You are far from stepping into your destiny, and you have lost hope from ever getting there.

Moving Forward

Why are you not moving forward? I believe there are two reasons. There are two things necessary for you to be healed and fulfill your destiny. First, you must want to be healed. Second, you must be willing to do whatever it takes to be healed. Stop performing, stop acting, stop pretending to be the perfect wife, accomplished husband, or best parent. Come out of denial, humble yourself, and acknowledge your need for healing. Choose to trust your heavenly Father to have your best interest at heart. Take His outstretched hand and walk with Him into your pain, into the hidden and dark corners of your being. Together you can do it. He will be right there with you so you will come out healed and free on the other side. And then you will joyfully dance together into your long-awaited destiny.

I believe many great destinies and exploits for God never came to be because men and women called to greatness were stuck in their healing process. The enemy knows our destinies, and he is scared of us entering into them. He is trying everything he can to keep us away, to keep us in bondage, so we are unable to fulfill God's will for our lives. The greater your destiny, the more he will try to get you out of the way. The deeper you have been hurt, the more horrible your life has been, the greater your destiny probably is.

Satan knew that Moses would deliver God's people and take them to the Promised Land, and so he unleashed a horrendous killing spree of babies. But God! He saved baby Moses who eventually fulfilled his calling. Esther was chosen to save her people from genocide. When she was young, her family was attacked and killed. Satan failed to kill her at that time, and she grew up and stepped into her role as Israel's deliverer. The greatest terror in the kingdom of darkness was unleashed at the birth of Jesus. Satan hoped Joseph would leave Mary when he found out she was pregnant, he hoped that she would be disgraced and outcast in society due to her untimely pregnancy. He hoped the long ride on a donkey to register in Bethlehem would cause a miscarriage. He hoped that Jesus' birth in an unclean stable would kill Him. And when nothing worked, he unleashed another killing of babies, yet Jesus was saved. He tried over and over to take Jesus out, but Jesus fulfilled His destiny.

The first time Jesus spoke at the beginning of his earthly ministry, He proclaimed what He had come for, quoting from Isaiah 61:1-2:

> *The Spirit of the Sovereign Lord is on Me, because the Lord has anointed Me to proclaim good news to the poor. He has sent Me to bind up the brokenhearted, to proclaim freedom for the captives and release from darkness for the prisoners, to proclaim the year of the Lord's favor....*

Do you need good news for a change? He has it for you. Are you brokenhearted? He wants to mend your heart. Are you addicted to destructive things? He wants to set you free. Are you living in darkness? He wants to bring you into His wonderful light. This is your time! This is your year to start walking again; to walk toward your destiny, because you have allowed Him into the painful areas of your life, and He is slowly transforming you into the beautiful, carefree, joyful, radiant little child who will take His hand and walk with Him wherever He goes.

Scary Times

God has created you, He knit you together in your mother's womb (see Ps. 139:13), you were a precious thought on His mind that came true. It does not matter what you have heard, whether you were an "accident" in your parents' eyes and rejected by them. He chose you, He formed every part of you and is very proud of His handiwork. You are His beloved child, and He cannot help Himself but smile when He looks at you. He wants to show you off, telling everyone, "Look at this one—he is Mine, she is Mine! Isn't she, isn't he amazing?"

My parents married when they were young, and my mother was in the middle of her university studies. When I came along just a year after their wedding, it did not fit into my mom's plans very well. She was forced to interrupt her studies, and when my brother was born three years later, she abandoned her studies and her dream of becoming a school teacher. But God did not depend on my parents' approval for my birth. The enemy was already at work trying to abort my destiny. When it was time for my birth on May 14, 1973, my little body became stuck in the birth canal and had to be pulled out. By the grace of God, I was a healthy though quite underweight baby.

My father felt pressured into the marriage. He was, and is, a broken man who did not have an easy childhood. He also received much pressure from his in-laws since they were part of high society, and he was just a simple worker, not a musician. He stayed away from home more and more and had affairs with other women. There is no specific day when he left for good, but I was around five years of age when he did not "officially" live with us any more. My grandparents played a big role in my childhood, and I loved them very much. I was my grandfather's princess, but that did not stop my grandparents and my mother from accusing me of being "like your father" whenever they got upset with me. I hated when they did that.

I do not have any memories from the first five to seven years of my life, and very few from my years at elementary school. I do remember that I was somewhat of an outsider even back then. As soon as I had learned to read, I was constantly reading; sitting reading my book on the side of the school playground at break time while everyone else was playing, though there were occasions when I would also play with the others.

The day I started fifth grade, which is a big transition in the Austria school system, Mom fulfilled a wish of mine and bought me a little cat. I was so happy! I loved my cat very much, and had something who loved me back unconditionally.

At the age of 12 my life changed radically from one day to another. My mom had brought her boyfriend home once for dinner, though I did not understand that was what he was. Later, during a week away of skiing, I was talking to Mom on the phone and she asked me what I thought about him moving in with us. I said, "No problem"—words that haunted me for many years as I held myself accountable for all that happened during the following years.

My mom's boyfriend moved in with us in 1986, and hell on earth started for me. He changed the house rules and immediately established himself as the head of the house, with everyone having to obey him, no objections allowed. We were not allowed to eat by the little table in front of the television anymore—only he and Mom could. We were not allowed to put our feet on the table or the couch—only them. Everything had to be spotlessly clean, and every stain was blamed on me and my brother. He hated my cat, and when I had come back from my summer vacation, I was told that the cat had been put to sleep. I was totally devastated as my cat had been my only friend—I hated this man even more.

It did not take long before I became his favorite object of attack, as my little brother went along with everything. I, on the other hand, rebelled and defended myself when accused unjustly. I soon learned the hard way to keep my mouth shout. Any reply to his accusations set him off, and he had quite a temper. He would start shouting, using the vilest words, and threatening me, and at times slapping me in the face. I hated mealtimes. I stopped being there for breakfast, but had no choice for dinner, and so I had listen to him rambling about me, calling me fat, and other cruel things. I would just sit silently, eating a few bites, and waiting for dinner to be over. From time to time Mom tried to stop him from saying those things, but she was never successful. I tried to talk to her, but she always defended him, saying it was not easy for him to suddenly have two children live with him. I felt like she never listened or even tried to understand me. I felt totally abandoned, alone, and hopeless.

The weekends were worst, because he started drinking alcohol as soon as he came home in the early afternoon on Fridays. Whenever he was drinking, his tongue was even more loosened and his hand even faster to slap me. But holidays were worst, and I remember many tears pouring out of me at Christmas or on birthdays. But the most traumatic was one day when I inadvertently woke up my mom who was sleeping on the couch in front of the television. He lost it, and started hitting me. I succeeded in running to my room and jumped into my bed and under the covers. He followed me into my room, and stopped in front of my bed, pouring out insults and threats. I was trembling, hoping he would leave, and then broke out in sobs and tears. Every night I was crying myself to sleep. Every day I was wondering whether I should kill him or myself. Every day I was crying out to God to come and help me, but I did not know God.

Years later God showed me how Jesus was standing right there between my mother's boyfriend and me, protecting me. I saw the tears in His eyes as the tears ran down my face, and He felt the pain as much as I did. Though I became depressed and lonely, feeling like no one in the world cared about me or loved me, I was not really alone. I just did not know it. I had one friend in school who I wrote little papers with, sending them back and forth during class, and that interaction with her plus my journal writing provided a way to vent and stay alive. My teenage years were the darkest of my life; I was effectively robbed of those important formative years of every person's life.

Every night I would utter a sigh of relief when my mom and her boyfriend disappeared into their bedroom at around 8 P.M. as the main program on television was starting at 8:15 P.M. It was my time to sit down in front of the television, dive into the fictional world displayed, and go to the kitchen to finally have a chance to eat without being accused of eating too much or being fat.

I had to devise strategies to not get caught with food. There was a corridor from the living room to their bedroom, and the bathroom was in that corridor right by the living room. Whenever one of them had to go to the bathroom, they could see me in the living room. So I learned to keep the volume of the television down and always have an ear toward the bedroom door. Unfortunately there were times when I was caught and had to pay the price for my rebellion. To this day I jump when I'm alone in somebody's house and someone walks in without me expecting it.

Though I became depressed and lonely, I was not really alone. I just did not know it.

Looking for Love

In school, the only subject was boys as I entered into teenage years with elevated hormone levels. I had a subscription to a teen magazine, and to this day I am amazed at how there were no taboos when it came to the subject of sexuality. As a teenager, the only longing of my heart was to be loved, and those magazines fed right into that hole of my heart, telling me all about sex with boys, with yourself, and anything else you could think of. I "learned" much about which I now wish I had stayed ignorant.

When I was 15 years of age, I spent one month on a language vacation in France, and my host family had pornographic videos in their living room. Out of curiosity, I put one in when I was alone at home, but I was totally disgusted by what I saw and quickly turned it off. The damage was done.

All my classmates were sharing about their first sexual experience, whether it was just kissing or going all the way, and I felt left out as the only one without a boyfriend. I felt totally ugly, reinforced by Mom and her boyfriend's words, and understood why I could not find someone to love me; still I kept hoping and searching. Yes, I fell in love with out-of-reach boys quite a few times, but it never went beyond dreaming.

At 15, I started going to dancing school. Even as a little girl I had longed to dance, but had been told I was too fat. Now my moment had finally come.

My first dancing course was the Mambo, which was the big craze as *Dirty Dancing* had just been released in movie theaters. The problem with ballroom dancing is that you cannot do it alone; you need a partner, and the dancing schools always had more girls than boys enrolled. My dancing career started at that time and lasted until I came to know the Lord five years later. I took lessons for all the ten dances of ballroom dancing, the Mambo and Lambada, all the Rock'n'Roll classes including acrobatics, and tap dance. I was part of two dance groups and performed a few times with those groups. I also attended many balls in the beautiful, white dress I had, but often went to those balls all alone.

I was a natural when it came to dancing and often learned the steps without having danced once all night. The guys would choose the girls to dance with, and I would not get picked. When it was time to switch, I hated breaking up the couples and seeing the disgust on the guy's face. So I preferred just watching and walked home from dancing school very sad and lonely many times. I did end up having dancing partner who I had to share with another girl, and at the end of the three years of dancing school I found a guy who then went on to start training with me to dance in competitions. He was also the one doing Rock'n'Roll acrobatics with me, even though he had a girlfriend. In spite of all these challenges, I loved dancing with a passion, and was really good at it. My spirit was always lifted when I got to dance, and I felt like I was coming alive.

Dancing took me out of the house, and I added many other things to my schedule. I wanted to be at home as little as possible to avoid being in the same place as my mother's boyfriend. I became extremely active and busy, and loving it all, and continued that way once I became a believer. I discovered that being busy was a great way of keeping myself from facing reality and keeping the pain away.

My busyness also allowed me to meet a lot of people, always in hopes of finding "the one" who would love me and fill the void inside of me. I was 17 when I went once again to a fancy ball by myself. I was standing by the dance floor all alone, wondering how long I would stay before going home, when a young man came up to me and asked me to dance. We ended up staying until the very end of the ball at 5 A.M., dancing and talking. I felt like I was coming to life.

That young man became my first boyfriend, and our relationship lasted seven months. My dream had come true, and I expected him to fill the void in my life. He could never spend enough time with me, love me enough, and our progress in the sexual arena was way too slow for me. My soul was filled with the content of the teen magazines I read of how the sexual act is the best thing there is in the universe. But it was not meant to be, as he broke up with me, and my world crumbled. I had just graduated from high school.

During all those years of darkness, two things kept me from trying to commit suicide. One, I believed in God. As a nominal Catholic, I knew that suicide was a deadly sin that God would not appreciate. Second, I did not want to die a virgin, and it seemed my only goal in life was to lose my virginity as quickly as possible.

I succeeded half a year before I came to know the Lord. I was 19, and it was New Year's Eve. This was the only time I ever experienced the loosening effects of alcohol. I had only just met the guy and did not even like him, but did not care when the kissing led to more in the bathroom of the apartment where we were invited. The act was totally unglamorous, nothing like I had read about, and the few more times we did it during the six weeks we stayed together were not any better.

A Beautiful Act of Love

The sexual union between a man and a woman has been instituted by God for marriage, and marriage alone. It is, in fact, a spiritual act when man and woman become one. It is a beautiful act of joy and fulfillment in marriage that is unique and very special. God has created it for us to enjoy, yet the world has totally perverted this beautiful and holy act and made it something vile and disgusting, perverting it to unspeakable acts.

Maybe you have tried, like me, to fill the hole in your heart with boyfriends and sex, only to find out that it did not work. The happiness is just temporary and fleeting, not giving you the fulfillment you are looking for. After becoming a believer, I was glad for a while that I got that over with before I was not allowed to do it any more, but it did not take long before God started filling me with His truth. I started grieving deeply over having lost my virginity, and just months before coming to know Him. I asked Him many times to forgive me, and He did.

Maybe you feel like you have had too many sexual partners to be forgiven. Maybe you feel like there is no hope for purity and restoration for you. I have good news for you today—women and men—God forgives you. And not only that, He is the One who restores all things, and He can even restore your virginity to you. In His eyes, you are pure, holy, having been washed by the blood of Jesus, wearing the white garment of His spotless Bride He is so in love with. He has thrown your sin into the deepest sea. It is as far away from you as the east is from the west, and cannot be brought back. Do not listen to your accuser who will try to remind you of your sin. Listen to the Lover of your soul who sees His beautiful, adorned Bride in her white garment of purity.

Starting the Healing Process

After I committed to following Jesus the rest of my life at the age of 20, I was on a honeymoon for a while. I had stopped existing and had started living. For the first time I experienced what real love and joy and peace was. I had not found love anywhere while growing up, but now there was One who loved me unconditionally. One who loved me so much that He gave His life for me, even before He knew whether I would accept His sacrificial gift. What love! I was actually asked by someone during that time whether I was in love, because I was glowing so much. Oh yes, I was very much in love!

I continued my lifestyle of being very active, now throwing myself into ministry as well, working with the Christian student group and investing myself at church, as well as doing all the other stuff. My life had changed dramatically. I was amazed at how the hate for Mom's boyfriend had turned into love, and knew only God could do that. I had such a longing to help others in desperate situations similar to mine, and testified to the Lord's transforming power in my life on many occasions. I remember when I gave a public testimony just over a year after having come to know Jesus, and God's hand of grace rested on me so visibly, touching those who were listening.

God had taken off the first layer of the onion, but I had no clue how many more layers there were, as unbeknownst to me He had barely scratched the surface yet. Some layers were thicker than others, and the healing process had barely started. We all need healing—some more than others—and I doubt we will ever be completely healed before we leave this earth. The important thing is that we continue in our healing to become more and more functional and free to do God's will.

I lived in Paris my first half year as a believer, which was the grace of God as I really needed time to grow, away from my family. I went home for Christmas, which was extremely tough, as it was as bad as it had always been. When I returned from Paris to live in my mom's home, it was very difficult. I put a lot of effort in guarding my heart and trying to love her boyfriend, but wasn't that successful. I had to continue listening to his insults, but at least he wasn't slapping me any more, and his alcohol consumption had been reduced dramatically due to health issues. Still, there were times when I had to flee the house and find refuge with friends.

I really wanted to find my own place and not have to live defensively any more. He encouraged that, telling me over and over how happy he would be the day I moved out.

When that day finally arrived in 1995, I was not even allowed to take my bed with me that I had slept on all of my life. The accusations of taking advantage of them did not cease, as I had no water in my apartment and went to their place once a week for a bath and to do my laundry. Every time I walked up to their apartment door, I pleaded the blood of Christ over me and prayed for protection; there were many occasions when I left there in tears, relieved to be going home.

A year after starting my life with Jesus, I first heard of the "Toronto Blessing" while in England where it was big news in the secular newspapers as it had just started to hit churches in England. Later that year, the first book on it came out; I bought it and devoured it. While reading testimony after testimony of the Father meeting His children and healing them, my heart started to burn with longing to experience the same. I knew I needed much healing, and most of all I wanted to experientially know the Father's love. I had no idea what a father was supposed to be like, and I so longed to find out.

In February 1996 I went back to Bournemouth where I had been the previous summer. I was responsible for the partnership between the Austrian student group and the southern English student groups, and so I had the joy of using my administrative gifts to organize this trip. I also added a few days to my time in England to spend with friends. The move of God's Spirit had also come to the church in Bournemouth, transforming many churches with His love. I heard about a citywide "Catch the Fire" meeting and was excited to have the opportunity to attend. I had high hopes of encountering God and being healed emotionally. At the end of the meeting, they started praying for people, and it looked like a battle field with people lying everywhere. I had never seen anything like it. I was also prayed for, but nothing happened. I was very disappointed, and felt like God didn't care.

Do Not Give Up

How many times have you felt the same way? How many times has God disappointed you, not meeting your expectations? Have you given up on even bringing your hopes up again? *Do not give up.* God has heard you. He has heard every one of your cries, and He cares very much. We do not know what is happening in the invisible world even when there is no manifestation in the visible.

The following day, I went to the service at a church I had previously been to and was totally stunned at the transformation I saw. God's presence was so strong, and everything centered on Jesus. I had come with a very different attitude, telling God, "I don't care whether You touch me or not, I love You anyway and want to praise You tonight." During the sermon, a verse the pastor quoted spoke straight to my heart:

> *So do not throw away your confidence; it will be richly rewarded.*
> *You need to persevere so that when you have done the will of God,*
> *you will receive what He has promised* (Hebrews 10:35-36).

My heart was lifted even more. At the conclusion of the service, there was a ministry time, and as I was prayed for, I fell to the ground for the first time in my life. It was the most wonderful experience!

Do not throw away your confidence. Do not stop hoping. It is darkest before the dawn. Persevere, and you will reap His promises to you. Maybe you have been prayed for an issue 100 times. Well, go get prayer 101 times. Do not give up. The day of your freedom and healing will come, and it might just be tomorrow.

As I lay on the floor with God working deeply inside of me, the forces of darkness at work in my life were stirred up, and the demonic started manifesting, speaking lies to me and making me feel uncomfortable. That day was the true beginning of my healing process.

Two months later, Claudio Freidzon came to Vienna for a big conference. I was more than ever aware of the need of healing from my past, and went there asking even more to set me free so I would be more effective for Him. The Lord did an amazing work in me at that conference. He filled me with His presence more than ever before, and I went down under His power with the word "glory." I left there a new person, more in love with Jesus and with His Word, and proclaiming in my newsletter that I was free. However, it was just another wonderful layer of healing. But let us not despise the small beginnings, and even the smallest miracle of healing is huge and reason to glorify God.

Over the next year and a half I went to every conference I could find in Europe. I went to Switzerland twice, and once to England, and every time I went with a deep hunger to know God more, and to be healed more fully. I also went with high expectations, and the Lord filled my hungry heart and took off more layers. I would get prayer at the end of the meetings, and would spend many hours on the floor with the Lord, often one of the last ones to get up. Sometimes those were amazingly precious times with God, but many times it was also very painful as He went in to tackle another area in my life where I needed healing.

There was a lot of pain, but I knew it was necessary for healing, and so I continued offering myself up to the great Physician. I was still looking to know God's love experientially, and as the barriers in my life that kept His river of love away came more and more down, more and more of His love could trickle through into my life. I also longed to be able to truly laugh, as it seemed I had never known what true joy or laughter was, and I saw tiny improvements there.

Freedom

In the beginning of 1996, a brochure for a healing and counseling school in Canada fell into my hands, and it immediately gripped my heart. I started dreaming about going there, and taking steps into the direction. It seemed absolutely impossible, but I kept dreaming. And God made the impossible possible. In September I got on a plane headed to Canada—crossing the Atlantic for the very first time—and fulfilling my dream of being trained to help people more effectively. Or so I thought. In reality, God sent me there to complete a big part of my own healing. I had no idea what I was getting myself into.

I had the most amazing and intense ten weeks in Kelowna, British Columbia. There were about 50 students living on campus, having classes every day, with a different ministry coming in every week to share their healing ministry with us. There were also times of ministry and small groups. I was so hungry for healing and restoration and did not care what it would take, how much pain it would take, or what other people would think. I just wanted the Lord, and I wanted freedom. I am not a middle ground person; I go for either everything or nothing.

And the Lord honored my desire and my willingness for Him to operate in my life and started a deep work in me just days into the school. For seven weeks I was in the fire of cleansing and purification, and on His altar—His operating table. There were moments of deep anguish, embarrassment (but I did not care), dying, coming out of denial, and reliving traumatic events of my childhood. There were tears, fears, panic, but also His healing balm and healing love that He poured out on me. At the end of the ten weeks, I was told I was one of two amazing testimonies.

After the first seven weeks, there was a conference at the church—it was truly a turning point for me. It was the moment of being set free completely. Words cannot describe what happened that weekend. I could not help but shout "freedom" over and over again, and the Lord's anointing was so strong on me, I could not even stay on my feet. This went on for hours, and it continued the remaining three weeks I was there. Then the Lord released me to dance before Him with flags. I had seen people do it, and longed to do so myself, but had too much fear of

YOU can CHANGE the WORLD

men and need of healing in my life. After being set free, I grabbed a flag and danced with all my might before the Lord.

Before returning to Austria, I attended my first Rodney Howard-Browne meeting where I was prayed for. Then there was a conference at a church near Vancouver that some of us students attended. At the end of the meeting, I was lying on the floor while the ministry was going on all around and could not even move my body because the anointing was so heavy on me. I just enjoyed His beautiful presence. After everyone else was gone, my friends came over to help me up. As soon as they lifted me off the ground just a little bit, I started to laugh and laugh and laugh, and could not stop. Everything was totally hilarious. They kind of dragged me to the car so we could go for lunch.

At the evening meeting, the exact same thing happened again. It was like my newfound freedom was sealed that day. Ever since coming to Jesus, I had asked Him to teach me to laugh. That day He answered that prayer. Ever I since that day I can laugh, and I enjoy laughing very much. Laughter is the best medicine (see Prov. 17:22). I often found in my life that God fills me with supernatural laughter to overflowing right after I have gone through a very difficult time when I never had any reason to laugh. I'm so thankful that our God is a God of joy and laughter.

When I returned to Austria, I was such a different person that I had to learn to live again, to live life as a healed person. People at church immediately saw the difference, and I was very glad when I was allowed to dance at church with my new flags. From then on until I left Austria a few years later, I danced during worship at every service, full of freedom for the audience of One.

Breaking Food Addiction

While a big chunk of my healing process was taken care of in Canada, there was still more. As a child and teenager, I had constantly been on diets due to being told I was fat, and my weight had gone up and down, but ultimately up more and more. After coming to the Lord, I knew that He loved me the way I was and that I did not need to lose any weight to earn His acceptance.

During my 40-day fast in 1997, I naturally lost a lot of weight and looked better than ever. My desire to honor God with my body arose again, and when I started eating again, I had to face the ugly truth that I had an eating problem. It was the first time I saw it as a real problem, and it was painful to face. I started offering this problem up to God, and He was helping me as I tried so hard to take good care of this temple of Holy Spirit (see 1 Cor. 6:19). However, we cannot do it in our own strength. And there is really no point in putting all our effort into changing behavior if we do not go to the root of the problem and tackle it there. And so I had little victories, but ultimately I was not really conquering the problem.

It was not until 2007 that the Lord heard my heart's cry and I finally made some progress. I went on a three-week fast that year, which renewed my desire to start eating healthy and lose weight. Instead, I failed miserably once again. But by this time, the Lord had given me tools, and I was not going to give up again. He orchestrated for me to have an inner healing session via Skype, and in that session the Lord went to the root of the problem. I saw myself standing in front of the fridge as a teenager, as I did so many times, looking for something to eat to medicate the pain inside of me, and eating and eating since nobody could throw in my face how fat I was and stop me. I asked the Lord for forgiveness, and His truth set me free that night. One little session had brought lasting freedom, and I lost 28.5 pounds in the following two months.

There have been ups and downs since then, and even more healing in the area of eating, but today I'm happy to eat healthy, and the right amount, and exercise, and keep losing weight to eventually achieve my goal weight. Today, I am the one controlling food; it is not the food controlling me. I could not do it; I did not have the strength to keep cutting off the ugly fruit when the problem was the root of the tree.

Why do you eat more than you should? Why can't you say no when you should? What is going on inside of you as you overeat? Allow the Lord to show you the root of the problem and set you free. If He could do it for me, He can definitely do it for you.

Fear of Marriage

While I was out to find a boyfriend in my teenage years, marriage was far from my mind then. When I came to know the Lord, I was not part of the crowd that thinks of nothing else but finding a mate. I was very happy being single with my Bridegroom, Jesus. I would tell anyone who asked that I did not care whether I would stay single or get married, whatever God wanted for me, whichever way I could serve Him best, was fine with me. And I meant every word of it.

However, in reality, I had a fear of marriage because I had never seen a good example of a couple in a healthy relationship. While in Canada, I saw a married couple fighting, and it freaked me out. All throughout my life I had the same recurring nightmare of my wedding day playing out like this. I was just about to walk into church in my white dress, and I panicked and ran away because I felt like I did not even know the person I was marrying. I was scared of being tied to another person forever without being able to get out.

The Lord first addressed this fear in 1998 when I finally admitted to myself that I had feelings for an African man in my church. This young man had revealed his feelings to me over the years; but every time he did, I went as far away as possible and kept my distance for a while. I had no intention whatsoever of marrying an African, seeing all the problems in mixed marriages, but I finally gave in and asked God for forgiveness. If He wanted me to marry an African, I would do so.

So I called him up right away and met with him and told him my feelings for him. He was very happy, but before we parted that night, he told me that while I was his dream woman and he had waited for this day for years, he was already engaged to an African woman. He basically told me I would have to marry him right away if he broke up with the other lady. That ultimatum tapped right into my greatest fear of marrying an unknown person. Africans marry first, and then get to know each other, while we Westerners do it the other way around. We decided to take a week to pray and seek counsel and then talk again.

I had a horrible week as the Lord showed me my fear of marriage, and helped me work through some of the issues. I also talked with leaders above me about the situation. At the end of the week, we met again, and he told me that he loved me and wanted to marry me, but that his engagement was set in stone and he would go ahead with it. That settled it! The wedding three months later seemed very hypocritical to me, but African ways are different.

During my time in Kansas City the Lord continued healing my heart of the fear of marriage. One day I was spending time with God at the International House of Prayer in Kansas City, when a man came up to me and simply said, "You are going to marry a preacher and travel around the world." When he walked away, the words hit me, and I knew God had spoken. Again, the fear of marriage was stirred up big time, and the Lord helped me deal with it a little more.

A year later I was given another prophetic word about my husband that stirred me up, and again there was more healing. By the time I left Kansas City for Mali in 2003, I had a desire to get married for the first time in my life and started praying for this man that God is preparing to be at my side.

Healing Sexual Brokenness

By the time I went to Mali, many layers of pain and woundedness had been taken off to reveal the beautiful woman God has created me to be. He had healed me to the point that He could send me all alone to a dark, Muslim nation, as a little girl at the hand of her big heavenly Father whom she had come to know intimately. While I was very much healed, there were still more layers to take care of. At the end of 2006, the Lord took my healing to the next level.

By that time, I was ministering regularly to the street children in Mali, and had taken the first few street children into my home half a year earlier, and it was not easy at all. I had had a fair amount of inner healing training in Canada as well as Kansas City, and applied it as best I could to help those boys, with limited results. I was crying out to God for a more effective way, and He answered my prayer. I had the opportunity to go to Ghana and take the basic course on Theophostic Prayer Ministry (TPM), which is the most effective tool I have found so far. During a session, images from my early childhood emerged that were disturbing.

Six weeks later, I went to the U.S. for a week of daily sessions, and more and more images of the first years of my life, that I had no recollection of, surfaced. I need to say upfront that there is no proof for any of those images truly being memories of what happened to me. The only thing I know is that the images were deeply disturbing and caused much pain as I relived those situations. And Jesus was right there to bring His truth, freedom, and healing. This was the beginning of my healing from seemingly horrible sexual abuse as a very young girl by my biological father, as I had TPM sessions whenever possible over the next few years.

Once again, my life changed for the better, allowing me to love more and have more patience for my African children. Not only could God choose a little, broken, Austrian girl who seemed the least suitable for this high calling, but He actually uses every horrible thing that ever happened to me for His glory. That is our God!

All our boys have been sexually abused, as well as beaten, abandoned, rejected, and feel like no one cares. I know how they feel. I know very well what they have gone through, and can empathize with them. I have much compassion and love for them and a testimony of hope so they know they can be completely free and healed and used by the Lord of glory to advance His Kingdom.

Have you been abused? Just come to your loving heavenly Father and let Him heal your heart. And then go and be a testimony of His healing power to those who need healing like you did.

~

Father, I thank You for loving me so much that You gently take me into Your arms to heal every part of my being. Thank You for healing my heart from all the pain and abuse of my past. Thank You for restoring me and making me into this beautiful vessel, worthy of a king, that can be used for His purposes and His glory even in

*the darkest and loneliest corners of the earth. Thank You for deliv-
ering me of all fear and breaking all bondage and addiction in my
life. Thank You for transforming me into a beautiful son or daughter of the Most High God who is forgiven, restored, pure, full of
light and love, and an image of Your Son Jesus. Hallelujah!*

Change Points

1. God is waiting for your permission to put the master key into the lock of your heart, and walk into the place of horror, the place of unimaginable pain, the place that you do not ever want to be reminded of ever again.

2. He is the One who restores all things, and He can even restore your virginity to you.

3. God has heard every one of your cries, and He cares very much. You do not know what is happening in the invisible world even when there is no manifestation in the visible—but God is with you always.

4. Allow the Lord to show you the root of the problem and set you free. If He could do it for me, He can definitely do it for you.

5. He actually uses every horrible thing that ever happened to you for His glory. That is your God!

Chapter Eight

Family Issues
and Forgiveness

Family Issues and Forgiveness

As mentioned previously, I longed to have a father, to have someone who loved me and truly cared for me, but every father figure had been a negative experience. My biological father left us to start a new life without looking back. I saw him once when I was 11 or 12, and once when I was 15. I made efforts to get in touch with him, but he didn't seem very interested. I finally gave up and decided to be happy without him in my life.

When I became a believer at the age of 20, the desire to know my dad reawakened. Knowing that there was possibly no interest on his side, I decided to be creative. A year and a half after I had come to know the Lord, I gathered all my courage, bought a gift, and went to my father's house. Nobody was home, and I was disappointed; I left the gift on his doorstep. Of course, he never called or wrote to acknowledge his gift.

A few months later I started writing daily postcards to him. On the blank side, I wrote one letter each day, while writing a little bit about me on the other side. If he placed the cards next to each other chronologically, he would read the sentence, "I love you and want to see you." As I neared the end of the sentence, I proposed a day, time, and location for us to meet. I was there, but he didn't show up. I was disappointed, but did not give up. I continued writing and proposed a new date to meet. Two weeks after the failed meeting, I met my dad at an ice cream shop. I was 22 years old.

Fathers

We did a lot of talking that day, and I heard my father's side of the story. My heart went out to him, and I longed for him to get to know Jesus. I openly shared my faith with him, but he rejected it. I had high hopes that this would be the beginning of a relationship. Two weeks later I met with him again and got to know the woman he was about to marry. I really liked her. I was hopeful, but my hopes were again dashed. I am still the one who has to go to great lengths to try to meet with him. Most of the time, he says he's too busy.

But I have good news! "A father to the fatherless, a defender of widows, is God in His holy dwelling" (Ps. 68:5). I am not fatherless anymore. I have the best Father in the whole universe. I do not have to run after my heavenly Father; rather, He runs after me with passion. I do not have to work hard to hear from Him; He talks to me all the time. He always has time for me. He constantly wants to spend time with me. He always listens, always cares, and always takes care of me. As soon as I call upon Him, He is right there to meet with me.

My earthly father hurt me, but my heavenly Father heals me. My earthly father has rejected me, but my heavenly Father has chosen me. My earthly father wanted to feed his own pleasure with me, my heavenly Father feeds me with His heavenly, holy pleasures. He truly loves me with an unconditional, everlasting love, and nothing I do or say can ever change that. He rejoices over me, He is proud of me, and He wants to show off His beautiful, precious, little princess to everyone around. He loves to have fun with me, to dance with me and play with me. He loves to protect me, even from the dangers that I am unaware of, and He loves to teach me and lead me on the perfect path.

My heavenly Father wants me to reach my full potential, and lovingly does everything necessary for me to get there. He is the perfect Father. He is the type of father He wanted me to have on this earth. But my earthly father failed because he is a broken man who could not be the man and father he needed to be because he never got to know the heavenly Father who was waiting for him to come into His family so he could be healed and restored and find love, joy, and peace in this life.

I have a lot of compassion for my earthly father, and pray that the day of his salvation will not stay a dream of mine but become reality. God is in the business of healing family relationships. "He will turn the hearts of the fathers to their children, and the hearts of the children to their fathers..." (Mal. 4:6 NKJV). I have shed many tears in prayer for my family—my father, mother, brother, grandparents—and have yet to reap the fruit of not being the only believer in my family. I rest in knowing that He loves them more than I do, and will not let those prayers go unanswered.

When I came to the Lord, I knew I had no idea what a true father was like, and over and over again I asked the Lord to reveal His Father's heart to me. Reading about "The Father's Blessing" in Toronto, my heart's longing grew more and more to know the Father not just in my mind but experientially. At every conference, the Lord would do more and more to answer this prayer. Today I cannot pinpoint a specific event when He gave me full comprehension of Himself as my Father. On many occasions I had encounters with the Father, visions of my Father, that brought healing and experiential knowledge of His immense Father's love for me. In early 1996, He showed me the following:

> Jesus stood beside me. I then felt like a little child again who only wanted to be loved—and I saw God the Father at some distance. So I ran into the arms of God, saying like a little child, *"Nobody wants me, they don't love me, Daddy!"* I saw my family standing at a distance, but I was safe in the arms of God. He was there to listen to me and hold me in His arms, and I didn't want Him to stop embracing me. You know, one of the things I had always wanted most in my life, was to be hugged by my mom (or anybody else), and most of the time she had only pushed me away when I had dared to just do it (quote from *News from Vienna 11*).

It might very well have been after my ten weeks in Canada that I was finally able to say for the first time that I truly knew my heavenly Father's love for me.

During my two years in Kansas City, the revelation of my Father's love for me went so much deeper as I spent countless hours in His presence, basking in His love. And then the Lord gave me the gift of an earthly father, one of my Bible school professors—healing my heart even more in the process now that I had a dad "with skin on." There was now someone who cared, someone who was available, someone who had my good in mind, and it blessed me tremendously. That relationship ended after about a year and left a lot of pain in the wake. The fault did not lie with him or me or his other daughters, but that did not make any difference when it came to the pain. As I boarded the plane to Mali, I was fatherless again—however, my heavenly Father was there, and He was never going to leave me or forsake me. He was right by my side as I sat in the plane and as I landed in this new land He had chosen for me. I continued walking with His hand in mine, and He was all I needed.

In early 2007, God once again gave me the gift of an earthly father. God had spoken to him that He was entrusting me to him as a daughter. Even though he was on the other side of the world, we talked via Skype about once a week, truly caring about me the way a biological father would. God used this man to show me what an earthly father was supposed to be like, and over time I started to believe that he truly cared for me with God's love the way an earthly father was meant to. But this father was also only given to me for a season, and the relationship was brutally ended after about ten months, and again due to no fault of either one of us. It was one of the most painful experiences of my life. Again, I had to fall into my heavenly Father's arms—who would never leave me or forsake me. The only One who would always be there for me, and always love me, and whose words were always true.

My Daddy in Heaven is my everything. I am so proud of Him, and He is proud of me. And I'm believing Him to give me fathers and mothers on this earth again, because "God sets the lonely in families" (Ps. 68:6). Jesus said, "And everyone who has left houses or brothers or sisters or father or mother or children or fields for My sake will receive a hundred times as much…" (Matt. 19:29). I have left everything, and He has given me brothers and sisters and many children. His promise is for the here and now.

The apostle Paul said to the Corinthians, "Even if you had ten thousand guardians in Christ, you do not have many fathers…" (1 Cor. 4:15). Where are the fathers and the mothers in the Body of Christ? Where are those who will be fathers and mothers for a generation of fatherless children? We need the fathers. We need the mothers. God has instituted that they would play a big part in the children's lives. There is an emptiness in those who have to grow up without a mother or a father; we all need parents "with skin on."

As a young person, I tell the older generation: We need you. In Austria, the older generation is totally absent from our few churches. I was so blessed to see every generation represented in churches in the United States. Men and women of God with much life experience and wisdom, who have so much to give to the younger generation, rise up and become a mother, become a father, to those who so need you today. Only then will the church turn from a dysfunctional family into a functional family that can do great exploits for God.

Families

In 2009, I had the joy of going to a meeting where my friend spoke about our wonderful heavenly Father. In the past, I used to be miserable as the pain of not having a father would get so intense. But that time was long gone, and instead I got more and more excited and giddy as I spent time thinking of how wonderful my heavenly Daddy is. When I think of Him, I become a little carefree girl full of joy.

And then I had a vision that came unexpectedly.

I saw myself as a little girl, maybe 4 years of age. There was a transparent wall right in front of me, and on the other side of the wall I could see a large crowd of people—comprised of all the men who had abused me. It was a frightening sight; the number of men, as well as the men themselves, who had caused such horror in my life. I did not want the wall to come down since it protected me from them.

Then I saw Jesus, radiating, standing over there, and I wanted to be with Him. So the wall came down, and suddenly I was next to Jesus. I took His hand, and knew I was safe. Together we went over to the men, and then such compassion came into my heart as I looked at each one of them. I could see their brokenness, how much they needed God and healing, and I touched each one as we walked by, like a healing touch, a touch of prayer so God would touch their hearts and heal them. They were also looking at me, but with a look of knowing what they had done, a look of respect and awe because they saw me as the King's daughter, as the one I am in Christ. All I felt was compassion for them, and the desire to see them healed and free.

And then the crowd parted, and Jesus walked with me very pur-posefully forward. Once the view was unobstructed, I saw that the throne with the Father was ahead of us. Full of excitement and joy, I let go of Jesus' hand and ran to the Father, jumping onto His lap. I cannot tell you how much joy I felt! I sat on His lap, looking at His face, and He looked at me. I felt so much love for Him, and told Him I was His, that I was giving my everything to Him. I touched His cheek, and He cupped my face with His hands, and His eyes and actions spoke vol-umes. I knew how much He loved me and cherished me, His princess. Then I put my head on His chest, and I could hear His heartbeat. His chest was so big, His lap was so big, there was so much room! As I lay my head there, He enveloped me with His arms and stroked my hair. I simply enjoyed His heartbeat and embrace, never wanting to leave that place again.

That is the place to live from. That is the place for us to be. In the arms of our amazing heavenly Daddy, on the lap of our perfect Father. What a privilege to be His sons and daughters! What an amazing, wonderful mes-sage we have to take into a fatherless world of many lonely, broken peo-ple who want nothing more than to find someone who loves them for who they are.

Forgiveness

From the day I decided to follow Jesus, I knew the importance of forgiveness. Everyone has been hurt by people, and many still walk around with the pain that keeps them in bondage and keeps them from entering into our destiny. Jesus spoke very clearly about how important forgiveness is, "But if you do not forgive others their sins, your Father will not forgive your sins" (Matt. 6:15). You may be thinking, *You can't be serious, Jesus. If you only knew how much I have been hurt. I can never forgive* _____ *for that.* But what about you? Have you not sinned? Do you not have need for forgiveness?

Sin is sin; however big it is, it always separates us from God. If you want to be forgiven and be in right relationship with God, then you do not have a choice but to forgive. He has forgiven you so much—can you not extend the same grace to that person who has hurt you? "Bear with each other and forgive one another if any of you has a grievance against someone. Forgive as the Lord forgave you" (Col. 3:13). You do not punish the person with your unforgiveness who might be totally unaware of it; the person you are punishing is yourself, and you are carrying the consequences and the pain. You are allowing a bitter root to grow up inside you that poisons your whole being and causes trouble and defilement (see Heb. 12:15). At times, bitterness manifests in cancerous growths appearing in people's bodies, though I am not saying that every cancer is caused by unforgiveness. However, my own grandmother was extremely bitter, and I have no doubt that the cancer that killed her was caused by her inability to forgive.

The Lord tells us in Matthew 5:48 to be "perfect" just as our "heavenly Father is perfect." That is quite a high bar, Jesus! How could any of us ever reach perfection on this earth? He is not asking for our performance, for us to work ourselves to death for Him. The context is quite clear. We are perfect if we forgive and love our enemies. That is all it takes. But it might sound easier than it is.

In Hebrew thinking, an enemy is a friend you have not spoken to in three days. It takes a lot of humility to be the first one to seek reconciliation after you have had a fight with a friend. At the sports camp where

I got saved, I chose to be my friend's enemy because of her actions toward me, and I refused to talk to her. When I wanted to start a life with Jesus, I knew I had to reconcile with her. It was not easy, but I took the first step and asked her to be friends with me again. Her first reaction was, "I'll have to think about it." It was not quite the answer I had hoped for, but I had done my part. A few days later our friendship was restored, and I had started my life with Jesus. I had forgiven her, and He had forgiven me.

I had a lot of forgiving to do in my life. I chose to forgive Mom's boyfriend by an act of will, and that act was tested over and over again, with me choosing to forgive him frequently. Eventually the feelings followed. I also had to forgive Mom, my brother, Dad, and others; and finally, I had been the hardest on myself and had a hard time forgiving myself. But if God forgives me, how arrogant is it not to forgive myself? I am actually putting myself above God if I am not willing to do as He has done. By the grace of God, you can forgive yourself. Choose to forgive, do not worry about emotions, for they will follow eventually as you are healed more and more.

Jesus told a story about how essential forgiveness is, and it went like this:

> Then Peter came to Jesus and asked, "Lord, how many times shall I forgive my brother or sister who sins against me? Up to seven times?" Jesus answered, "I tell you, not seven times, but seventy-seven times. "Therefore, the kingdom of heaven is like a king who wanted to settle accounts with his servants. As he began the settlement, a man who owed him ten thousand bags of gold was brought to him. Since he was not able to pay, the master ordered that he and his wife and his children and all that he had be sold to repay the debt. "At this the servant fell on his knees before him. 'Be patient with me,' he begged, 'and I will pay back everything.' The servant's master took pity on him, canceled the debt and let him go. "But when that servant went out, he found one of his fellow servants who owed him a hundred silver coins. He grabbed him and began to choke him. 'Pay back what you owe me!' he demanded. "His fellow servant fell to his knees and

begged him, 'Be patient with me, and I will pay it back.' "But he refused. Instead, he went off and had the man thrown into prison until he could pay the debt. When the other servants saw what had happened, they were outraged and went and told their master everything that had happened. "Then the master called the servant in. 'You wicked servant,' he said, 'I canceled all that debt of yours because you begged me to. Shouldn't you have had mercy on your fellow servant just as I had on you?' In anger his master handed him over to the jailers to be tortured, until he should pay back all he owed. "This is how my heavenly Father will treat each of you unless you forgive your brother or sister from your heart" (Matthew 18:21–35).

Both these men were servants of the king who represents God. Jesus is not talking to unbelievers, but to Jewish believers, members of God's chosen people. The first servant had a huge debt with the king. Ten thousand talents would be about 2 or 3 billion dollars today—the wage of 165,000 years of work. How was he able to accrue that large of a debt? He must have lived way beyond his means at the king's court, and probably took the king's money and spent it on himself. Why hadn't anyone noticed earlier his lavish lifestyle? By showing off his status and wealth, he actually took glory away from the king he was supposed to serve and represent, and therefore dishonored him. The king was most gracious when he forgave him his debt, even after he lied about paying it all back, which he could have never done. That is the way our heavenly Father is! He forgives us a debt we do not deserve to be forgiven of, and a debt that we could never repay.

Consequences

But the servant had a very short memory of the amazing gift he had received. Are we not just like him? Do we not forget how much God has forgiven us, and hold our brothers and sisters accountable for the smallest debt? The second servant owed about $3,000 to $5,000—an amount that was not impossible to pay back eventually—but he received no mercy from the servant the king called wicked. The king did what was lawful, and threw the first servant into jail to be tortured. He had missed an occasion to pay forward the mercy he had received, and ended up where he had no more possibility to ever even start paying it back.

This story should make us aware of the severe consequences of unforgiveness. Not only are we called to forgive, we are called to love our enemies (see Matt. 5:44), those friends we have lost relationship with, "If you love those who love you, what reward will you get? Are not even the tax collectors doing that?" (Matt. 5:46).

My first year in Kansas City was heaven, while my second year was hell. But I thank God today for the dying that was going on and for all the precious life-lessons I learned through the difficult season I had to go through. In the beginning of 2003, the Lord spoke to me clearly that one new policy that my Bible school had implemented was going against all the school stood for, and was not His will. My heart was very troubled about this issue, and I finally told God I was ready to leave the school if necessary. I wrote a very polite and humble letter to the school sharing my heart, and the issue was amended by leadership. I was greatly relieved to be able to stay in school.

Still, things were not good at all. I did not even know what was happening. I found myself being considered rebellious and was isolated within the church together with a little group of students and one teacher who ended up stepping down. People started avoiding us, and sermons were preached that were clearly directed against us. My heart was breaking, wondering whatever I had done to deserve this treatment. I loved the church, I loved the pastors, and I had no intention of becoming disloyal to them. However, that was what I was accused of. Unfortunately there was never a personal conversation, but everything happened behind our backs and from the pulpit.

People left the church in the process, many deeply hurt in their hearts. As for me, my two years of school were coming to an end anyway. I felt totally cut off and ostracized and received my diploma without any hope of being ordained or sent out with a blessing. The pastors would not even talk to me. I was deeply hurt and felt I had been treated unjustly.

It would have been so easy to just turn my back to the church and never go there again, acting the way a child would—if they don't want me, I'll go. I could have let the pain fester, let a root of bitterness grow up, and become angry with church leadership on the whole, not stepping into any church again. Unfortunately, some of the people who were hurt reacted just like that, and it hurt my heart to see them live in bondage to their pain.

However, I chose to forgive them. I chose to continue to love them, no matter what. Every time I came back to town, visiting from Mali, I visited that church. I tried to talk to the pastors. After a few tries, I met with the pastor's wife for the first time, and told her how thankful I was for everything that the church had put into my life. I told her that they had a part in all the fruit I was seeing in Mali and around the world. I was even in tears as I loved her so much, and wanted her to know that.

Every time I came back, I did the same, sharing what God was doing in Mali. Then one time the pastor himself heard me share my heart of thankfulness and gratefulness and love for them. I testified how much the school prepared me for what I am doing today. And then they started supporting the ministry financially. My persistence in loving them and letting them know I loved them paid off. Forgiveness first flowed only in one direction, but hearts submitted to our Lord cannot resist forever, and so my love melted the resistance until forgiveness was returned and relationship was restored. What a powerful testimony of the love of God!

Choose Today

Is there anyone who has hurt you, but you have not forgiven him or her? Choose today to take the first step in forgiving that person. Not only that, but start showering your love on that person. "If your enemy is hungry, feed him; if he is thirsty, give him something to drink. In doing this, you will heap burning coals on his head" (Rom. 12:20). Remember that an enemy is a friend you have not talked to. Your love will melt the unforgiveness your friend has toward you. Our God is a God of forgiveness and restoration of relationships. He wants us to live in peace and harmony with all men as much as it is up to us (see Rom. 12:16; 1 Pet. 3:8).

Imagine a church without bitterness and enemies. That would be a sight to glorify God and draw the unbelievers in as they would see the love we have for each other (see John 13:35). His Bride would be one big step closer to being "without stain or wrinkle or any other blemish, but holy and blameless" (Eph. 5:27), ready for the great wedding day to come.

Healing for your heart is absolutely crucial as you prepare to become a world changer. However broken you are, however messed up you are, nobody is too broken to be mended and healed and transformed into a vessel God can use for His glory. The first step is wanting to be healed and set free. God will work within your boundaries, and not heal you if you are not truly willing. If you want to be free from addictions, bad habits, thoughts, or other issues that have a hold on your life, Jesus has come to set you free and is waiting for you to come to Him.

If you do not know what joy is, there is fullness of joy in His presence. If you are plagued by fear, His perfect love casts out all your fear. If there are people in your life you hold a grudge against, release them, forgive them and find freedom from this bondage. If you do not know what a true father is like, come to your heavenly Father and find out. If you have been abused in any way, let your perfect Father gently heal your heart and soul. If you do not know what love is, what it means to be loved, there is One who not only loves you but who is Love itself. His arms are outstretched wide. He is waiting for you to come to Him, so He can shower His healing and blessings upon you. Are you ready to open your heart to Him? Then pray with me:

> *Precious Father, I forgive* _____
> *for having hurt me so deeply, and I ask You to show me ways to shower love on him or her. I thank You for everything You have forgiven me, and I choose to walk in total forgiveness at all times. I want to know You intimately as my heavenly Daddy, not just intellectually, but in the depths of my heart. Take me into Your arms, let me jump onto Your lap, and let me gaze into Your eyes, seeing the immense love You have for me. Thank You for never forsaking or abandoning me, but for always being at my side, holding my hand, and walking on the path of life with me together. I love You so much, Daddy!*

Change Points

1. God runs after you with passion. You do not have to work hard to hear from Him. He always has time for you. He constantly wants to spend time with you. He always listens, always cares, and always takes care of you.

2. Your heavenly Father is there for you, and He is never going to leave you or forsake you.

3. It takes a lot of humility to be the first one to seek reconciliation after you have had a fight with a friend.

4. Your love will melt the unforgiveness your friend has toward you. Your God is a God of forgiveness and restoration of relationships.

5. If you do not know what a true father is like, come to your heavenly Father and find out.

Chapter Nine

Divine Enabling and Encounters

Divine Enabling and Encounters

You know your destiny; you have gotten rid of all sin and impurities in your life; you have humbled yourself and died to self; you have renounced all unforgiveness; and, you have found healing from the painful events of your past.

You say, surely now I am ready to change the world!

Not quite.

Two things are still absolutely essential before you step into your destiny. Jesus said, "I am the vine; you are the branches. If you remain in Me and I in you, you will bear much fruit; apart from Me you can do nothing" (John 15:5). First, you need to have an intimate relationship with your God; and second, you need to be equipped with divine power to do the works that Jesus did. The second flows out of the first.

Power and gifts without intimacy are deadly, as history has proven over and over again. Once you find intimacy, the gifts are not even such a big deal anymore. It's simply natural that they flow through you because you have been with the Lover of your soul who is also the Creator of the universe. Miracles are natural and normal when you live at His hand, doing only what you see your Father do (see John 5:19), and not what you yourself want to do. How can miracles not happen if they are on God's heart, and He is the One who told you to do them? How have miracles even become such a big thing? Why it is all that some people run after? Jesus already said, "A wicked and adulterous generation looks for a miraculous sign" (Matt. 12:39, Luke 11:29). Miracles are a natural outflow of our relationship with God and should not be seen as something extraordinary, even though we thank God for every single one of them.

When we start our lives with Jesus, we acknowledge His lordship and dedicate ourselves to serving Him the rest of our lives. It is a beautiful thing to have such a wonderful Master, who is always just and treats us right. But we were not created to become hard workers for God. Our purpose in life is not to work as hard as we can for His Kingdom to please our Master.

When I came to know Jesus, I simply continued doing what I did before, but now I worked hard for Jesus instead of the world. I loved Him so much, I just wanted to invest myself totally into Him and spent all my time being busy for Him. There is nothing wrong with working hard in His Kingdom. But He has not saved us so He has more workers to advance His Kingdom.

In John 15:15 Jesus makes a remarkable statement:

> *I no longer call you servants, because a servant does not know his master's business. Instead, I have called you friends, for everything that I learned from My Father I have made known to you.*

The disciples had left everything to become Jesus' servants. They became His students, striving to learn everything He knew until they would be rabbis in their own right. And then Jesus changes their relationship in this dramatic way, taking it to a new level. Their identity was not in what they did for Jesus, but in their love for Him, and intimacy they had with Him. They had spent countless hours together, getting to know each other really well. They did not need to prove anything to Jesus. They did not need to perform. They could simply sit down at the feet of Jesus and listen, enjoying His presence. True friends do not always need to talk. They can just sit together enjoying each other's presence. They know what the other likes or dislikes. And when their friend calls them in the middle of a huge crowd, they immediately recognize his voice. Jesus said, "his sheep follow him because they know his voice" (John 10:4).

Friends of Jesus

Are we His friends? Do we know Jesus' voice, able to distinguish it from the hundreds of other voices out there? Or are we only servants doing our jobs but have no access into the inner circle of our Master? It grieves my heart that we sometimes act as if He is the servant, and we are His master. We treat Him like a vending machine—put a prayer in and get the result that drops down—and then get upset when God does not give us the exact selfish wish we prayed for. When we rattle off our list of requests before His throne, our eyes are fixed on our list as we read it. We cannot see the longing in our Father's eyes who wished we would put down the list and just come up on His lap and spend time with Him, just gazing upon His beauty and enjoying Him.

It is time for God's people to become His friend, His lovers, those who just want Him. As you enjoy sitting in His lap and looking at Him, you are unaware that your Father dispatches angels to take care of your needs, without you ever having mentioned them (see Matt. 6:8). Do not even earthly parents act like this? When all my children in Mali do is ask me for stuff, I am not happy, and I do not want to give it to them. But when we spend a great time together without them asking for anything, I will give to them what I know they want, even without them asking for it. How much more does our heavenly Father love to pour out His blessings and gifts on us when we are simply His little children who totally trust Him and love to be with Him for who He is, and not what He can give us.

Delight in His Gifts

As we delight in Him, He gives us the desires of our hearts (see Ps. 37:4). And He is the One who put them there in the first place, if we put Him first in our lives. It is not wrong to desire spiritual gifts, as even the apostle Paul encouraged us to do so (see 1 Cor. 14:1). We need to be equipped with His gifts to accomplish the great tasks He has given us, which are nothing less than to change the world and advance His Kingdom. He knows exactly how each of us needs to be equipped so we are able to fulfill our calling. He puts natural talents into us while we are even in our mother's womb, and later equips us with supernatural gifts.

As a young believer I was sometimes ashamed of being talented in so many ways, able to do a great variety of things. I feared that people would see me as arrogant and look down on me. It took a few years before I realized that all my talents had come from God, and that He uniquely equipped me with them since I needed them to go to Mali all alone. There, I had to fill many roles—pastor, worship leader, preacher, administrator, Web designer, mother, and many other roles.

From the moment I started my life with Jesus, I had a great hunger for His Word, to get to know Him more, as quickly as I could. In January 1994, God responded to this hunger in a totally unexpected and amazing way.

I was approaching the end of my five months in Paris, and was invited to a healing seminar weekend at the charismatic Anglican church in the heart of Paris. At this point, I was rooted in the non-charismatic camp of church, but I had visited that Anglican church once before and liked the worship time. I did not know that this weekend would change my life totally. As we were worshiping God, His presence started filling me tangibly. We were singing Brian Doerksen's song "So Come" over and over, inviting Holy Spirit to come and fill us. Every time we sang the chorus, Holy Spirit filled me more. I had never experienced anything like it in my life. Months later I found the song on a CD, which became the first worship CD in my possession; it is still one of my favorites.

The weekend was full of things I had never witnessed before— words of knowledge and healing miracles. I was a little fearful of all these strange and unknown things but dared to attend one of the healing workshops. My hands started tingling as I was listening, which they said was a sign of the healing gift. I fled the room before I would have to do something weird. Even before I knew anything at all, and just as I was entering into the depths of what God had for me, God already started equipping me with hands to heal.

Holy Spirit's presence stayed with me as the preacher preached. At the end of his message, there was an altar call, which I had never witnessed before. My heart longed to respond and to be prayed for and receive even more of His presence, but the fear of others held me back as there were several of my non-charismatic friends who seemed somewhat critical.

People started leaving the room, and I knew the preacher would not keep praying for much longer. My desire for God finally won, and I went forward for prayer. I closed my eyes as the preacher prayed for me. Immediately God's presence multiplied considerably, even more as the preacher spoke in a language I did not understand. It was hard for me to remain standing, and I concentrated hard on that. Finally he walked away. After a short while, I returned to my seat, and was glad to be able to sit down. My legs were shaky, as my being was full of God's presence and glory. I felt like I was radiating with God's glory, and I was very hot. I was so overwhelmed by His love for me, and wanted to fall down in tears and adoration. This was the same weekend that God started moving in Toronto, Canada. He had baptized me in the Spirit without me even knowing anything about it.

His Presence

I went home and could not wait to feel the awesomeness of His tangible presence again. Not only that, but the tingling was also there for quite a while. My time of pure Bible study now turned into times of simply worshiping God as well.

I returned to Austria a week later, saying to God, *Surely there must be a church like this in Vienna.* Three months later, I went to Vienna Christian Center. The pastor was doing a series on the gifts of the Spirit, and I was so hungry to learn and grow and know more. I loved the church, loved the worship, loved the preaching, and would not miss a service from the first day on. I realized that I had received the gift of speaking in tongues when I was baptized in the Spirit, and now that I knew, I tried it out. I spoke a few words, but it was certainly a very weird experience to me. I thought I was making up the words, but in obedience I tried again and again. For one year I struggled with this gift, but I read book after book to understand better and learn. I kept asking God to give me total assurance that I was not making it up, and confidence that it was truly His Spirit speaking through me.

In the summer of 1995—two years after I had come to know the Lord and just over one year after starting to use the gift of tongues—I had one of the most extraordinary encounters with God. I was in Bournemouth, England, just about to start a two-week outreach with the Christian student group there. The girls were sleeping in the church I considered my church—the church where I had first been slain in the Spirit and had been totally transformed by God's love, thanks to the "Toronto Blessing."

Divine Encounter

The sanctuary was totally empty, with the chairs put away, and while the others went to bed, I sat at the piano and sang and worshiped, enjoying the big room to myself. I had a wonderful time with my God! On the second night there, I was praising God and singing to Him in the sanctuary. This is what happened:

> I was so full of love for Him and thanksgiving! After a short time, I suddenly fell forward to the floor. What was happening? I hadn't really fallen under God's power yet being with Him alone. So I lay there wondering and enjoying God's presence, wondering what would happen next. Suddenly God poured out His Spirit on me in an absolutely amazing way! Wave after wave of His love came on me, even increasing until I nearly had to say, *"Stop, it's too much!"* And then I started to sing in tongues in a way I never had before! It was so beautiful, and God was so close! I didn't want to stop. When I finally got up and went to bed, about one and a half hours had passed (quote from *News from Vienna 9*).

All doubt was gone after that; the Lord had even given me another language that was distinct from the first one. Since that day, I have been using this wonderful gift with much joy.

During the two-week outreach, I was able to hear God's voice as never before. Walking up to people on the street He told me to approach, I was absolutely blown away as He gave me insight into their lives. That's the way I wanted to live!

More, Lord!

Jesus said, "If anyone is thirsty, let him come to Me and drink" (John 7:37) and "whoever drinks the water I give them will never thirst" (John 4:14a). When you drink from His life-giving waters, you do not want to drink any other water. But as you drink His waters, your thirst for His waters will grow and grow. The more I drank from Him, the more thirsty I was for Him. "More, Lord!" became my heart's cry as I spent hours in His presence, longing for more of Him.

Every time I heard about a conference where I knew God would move powerfully, I longed to go and meet with Him, and many times I succeeded, going to England, Germany, and Switzerland at great expense, often fasting during part or all of the conference. When we are hungry for God, we do not care what it takes to find Him.

How much are you willing to give to meet with Him? How much worth does His presence have for you? If God wants to, He can meet with me right where I am. Of course, He can. But just maybe He is not going to give His presence away cheaply. Maybe He wants you to pay a price. The more we pay for something, the more precious it is to us, and the more we will take care of it. Maybe a few thousand dollars seems too much to pay to find God, and yet thousands flock to outpourings of God's Spirit when they become known.

Let's say I pay a few thousand dollars without knowing what I will get. After all, it's a risk buying something blind, going to an outpouring without knowing whether you will really encounter God. What if what you get is one little cucumber? You will be very disappointed. But what if what you get is a brand-new Porsche? Is a few thousand dollars still a high price to pay? No, you will be over the top about the great bargain. Meeting with God is multiple times greater than a new Porsche. It is

worth the price to be paid—financially, time-wise, and in terms of sacrifices to be made.

His Manifest Presence

At those conferences, I spent hours in His presence, lying on the
floor and enjoying His presence, often one of the last to get up. At those
conferences, God spoke to me, and equipped me with gifts. I had a
longing for the gifts of prophecy and healing, and again and again I
ended up being prayed for and was touched powerfully as the Lord increased those spiritual giftings in my life. Often my hands would be
burning as if on fire during healing meetings, and I had opportunity to
practice praying for the sick. Other times I had the opportunity to step
out in the prophetic as we prayed over each other. I was making baby
steps in these arenas, longing to grow.

In June 1996, I received my very first prophetic word in a public
meeting in Austria. I was surprised and totally blown away that God
would speak to me like that. Many more followed in Canada, and later
in Kansas City, and I'm eternally thankful that the Lord speaks through
His people to bring encouragement and confirmation.

The ten weeks in Canada, and specifically the last three weeks, were
a tremendous time of living in God's manifest presence. When God set
me free, not only could His love and tangible presence flow unhindered
in my life, but the gifts of prophecy and healing also increased, as the
fear of others melted away, and I was humbled and stunned and honored to be used by my heavenly Father to bless His children. I had been
in the ministry team at my church since its beginning in 1995, but
when I returned from Canada, God was able to use me more effectively
than ever before, and I loved it.

Every time I came back from a conference, I was full of God; and
every time I intended to stay that way, but every time I would keep leak-
ing, unable to continue living in His fullness. My heart would break as I
longed for nothing more than to live in His manifest presence at all times.
I was wondering whether it was even possible, but did not give up trying.

In the summer of 1997, James Goll came to Austria, and I had the opportunity to be at his seminar. He spoke about the importance of praying in tongues, and his stories gripped my heart. I was convicted of not using this precious gift enough, and started setting my alarm every day to pray continually in tongues for a specific amount of time. I increased that time slot more and more until I was up to 90 minutes of continual praying in tongues. By that time, I was attending an intense three-week English teacher training, and humanly speaking did not have time for praying that long. But the blessing coming out of it was extraordinary. I was strengthened supernaturally, and God used me to be a blessing to my fellow students. I wish I could say that I have continued doing this since.

How much time do you spend using this precious gift God has given you? Allow Him to edify you and refocus you as Holy Spirit prays through you.

His Holiness

In early 1998, I had another wonderful opportunity to be in God's presence for an extended period of time. A revival preacher came to Austria and kept extending his meetings. Even though I was busy at university and it was even exam time, my hunger for God kept drawing me. We would worship God for about an hour, and His glory would come down so that I was overcome by His presence, and I would spend the whole meeting on the floor—every time! It seemed the more I received, the hungrier I got. I did not care about anything but Him, dedicating my life completely to Him. Fear of man melted away. By the third week I was so drunk in the Spirit that my friends had to help me up and to the car. I was unable to talk as His holiness lay over me, and it would have seemed improper to. I had the most amazing three weeks of being filed, refreshed, edified, and equipped.

But once again, God's manifest presence decreased until it was gone again, and my heart was again empty and crying out for Him. However, God says, "I love those who love Me, and those who seek Me find Me" (Prov. 8:17), and I was not willing to give up. I kept believing that it was truly possible to live in His fullness and walk in His presence at all times.

I was out to prove those people wrong who believed me crazy. I would show them that God's Word is true that those who seek Him find Him.

At the end of 2000, I finished my university studies in Vienna. One day I saw a Charisma magazine lying open on my desk, and was immediately gripped when I saw Kansas City—where the Bible school was located that I had always wanted to attend. Then I saw two words that had been my calling and passion for years—nations and revival—*World Revival School of Ministry* (WRSM) in Kansas City. I knew that the "Smithton Outpouring" had relocated to Kansas City, and that the Lord had poured out His Spirit mightily in that place.

I could not shake the desire to go to that school. I prayed about which school to go to, and always came back to WRSM. I pursued both schools and churches; the dean of WRSM rarely wrote back or answered my questions, while the other dean answered every one. Still, I felt that God wanted me to attend WRSM. About a month before I left for the U.S., I knew for a fact that God had called me to WRSM. People thought I was crazy as I gave up my life in Austria and went to Kansas City without ever having been there, not knowing anything about it. God said, "Go and I will take care of all your needs." As Abraham had done thousands of years earlier, I left my homeland to go to a foreign and unknown land, having nothing but God's word to hold on to. I was leaving for God's Promised Land.

Arriving at *World Revival Church*, I was overwhelmed by the wonderful worship there, and loved the testimonies I heard. Pastor Steve Gray had just returned from Australia, and shared a unique message on the nations. I never heard him preach like that again. I was blown away as I listened and as the Lord confirmed to me that this was where He wanted me to be. I wrote:

> At the end, suddenly the whole church rushed—I mean, they RAN—as one to the front, without any call! God's power was there and He deeply touched me. I started to weep inside as He showed me how everything has led up to my being here and how this was IT, and how this would be the fulfillment of His promises. I was overwhelmed, felt so insignificant, so little, so unworthy and so honored to have

the privilege to be part of this. This inner weeping went on pretty long. Suddenly everything fit perfectly. I felt so much at home there, in the perfect will of God. (Quote from email newsletter June 12, 2001.)

For eight years I had been crying out for His presence, had been hungry for more of Him. And He had heard my heart's cry and had sent me to an oasis of His presence. I was overwhelmed with gratitude that I would now be able to live in His presence daily. While responding to previous altar calls was often linked with shame, because it was believed that a person should not have to go get prayer again, it was quite the opposite at my new church. You were expected to go get prayer after every service, and there were five services a week for a while. I was filled continually with His presence—at church, school, home—and my hunger was being satisfied and yet getting greater.

Ones Who Loved God's Presence

I love the example of Joshua in the Bible. Joshua was Moses' faithful assistant. One of the most powerful and overlooked verses is Exodus 33:11, "The Lord would speak to Moses face to face, as one speaks to a friend. Then Moses would return to the camp, but his young aide Joshua son of Nun did not leave the tent." We all know that Moses was God's friend and that he would meet with Him in the ten of meeting where the glory of God came down. But when Moses was done talking with God, there was one who did not leave. There was one who had tasted God's presence and could not get enough. Joshua would not leave the tent, he stayed in God's presence as long as he could. Joshua had great hunger for God, and God was pleased with him. He was able to make Joshua into Moses' successor, the one who would take God's people into the Promised Land.

Another example in the Bible of one who loved God's presence more than anything is King David. The Psalms are full of David's expressions of longing for God. Psalm 84:2 says, "My soul yearns, even faints, for the courts of the Lord; my heart and my flesh cry out for the living God." David even longed physically as well as emotionally and spiritually to meet with his Maker. He had only one wish:

One thing I ask from the LORD, this only do I seek: that I may dwell in the house of the LORD all the days of my life, to gaze on the beauty of the LORD and to seek Him in His temple (Psalm 27:4).

Can you join in David's prayer from the bottom of your heart? David still lived in the old covenant. We have a better covenant, and many of us do not even come close to where David was spiritually. He was a king, yet he was humble and wanted God more than a kingdom. He was not concerned about what people would say; he worshiped and praised God with everything in him, even dancing passionately in public. Can you compare with David? Or do you have to ask God to increase your hunger for Him?

Growing in the Prophetic

Upon arriving in Kansas City, I was looking forward to growing in the prophetic. I wanted to sign up for a class at *Grace Training Center*, but God would not allow it. He then made me aware that Jill Austin was teaching a prophetic class at the newly formed Forerunner School of Prayer within the *International House of Prayer*. I had never heard of IHOP before coming to Kansas City, but I had heard of Jill Austin and that she moved in the prophetic. I signed up for her class in obedience to God. I had no idea the amazing things God had in store for me.

My life was deeply impacted by the class. Jill had such a great hunger for God, such a passion for His presence and glory, and all she wanted was to be contagious, so she could reproduce herself and have many sons and daughters with the same hunger and passion for God. Every week, I would encounter God personally in a powerful way and leave more impacted, more filled, and more hungry. After a few weeks, she started saying that she would share her 21-day visitation she had had years earlier; she said that some of us would have a visitation ourselves.

On October 13, 2001, I lay down on my living room floor as always, opening my Bible to read His Word. It happened to be Second Chronicles 7:1-2:

When Solomon finished praying, fire came down from heaven and consumed the burnt offering and the sacrifices, and the glory of the LORD filled the temple. The priests could not enter the temple of the LORD because the glory of the LORD filled it.

Solomon had just dedicated the newly built temple to the Lord in prayer in chapter 6. I started reading the first verse, "When Solomon finished praying, fire..." That is how far I got. Suddenly God's fire came down from Heaven and hit me. His fire, glory, and power started shaking me to the core as He consumed me, the living sacrifice, on His altar. Whenever it subsided a little, I tried reading the verse again, but the simple word fire increased God's manifest power again. It took me 45 minutes to read that first verse.

For three hours I was shaking in God's presence, my temple being filled with His glory the way He filled the temple back then. I lost all sense of time and was so overwhelmed I could barely get up at the end of the three hours. When I went to church that night, I could not stay on my feet for very long, so I spent the whole service on the ground. As soon as I walked into the classroom at Bible school in the morning where worship was already taking place, I hit the ground again, and spent whole classes on the floor in His manifest presence.

When I went home, as soon as I walked into my apartment, His power was there again, consuming me, as I offered myself up to Him. In the middle of this amazing ten-day visitation I wrote:

> I've been doing deep intercession for Mali where my heart is, wearing my Malian clothes, and crying out to God to be transformed into the image of Christ, prepared for His service, consumed by Him and passionate for Him, not caring about anything else any more... I want to get even more desperate for Him, even more like Him, disappear so that His glory flows through me, so that His power flows through me, for Him to be glorified, honored in the nations, for His kingdom to come in all its power! I pray that nothing of me will be left so that His will can be done through my life! (Quote from email newsletter, October 16, 2001.)

My deepest heart cry was answered during those ten days. The Lord removed the last barrier for me to continually know His manifest presence. Every time I would come before His throne, Holy Spirit was there to spend time with me. He was always there to fill me afresh, to show me Jesus and the Father. I had always longed to have a relationship with the precious Holy Spirit, who was also very visibly Jill's friend. And He became my friend also. I had access to the Father by Jesus' sacrifice, walking in at the hand of Holy Spirit. A lifelong dream had come true. I had found the intimacy with God for which I had always longed.

Called to Enter Into His Glory

Too many believers stay in the outer courts of the temple, bringing the ritual sacrifices of cleansings, confession, and repentance, which are of course good. Every Jew had access to that court. People spent a lot of time there standing in line waiting for their sacrifice. But only the priests could go into the holy place. We, as believers, are all priests (see 1 Pet. 2). That day when Solomon dedicated the temple, the priests could not enter the temple because of God's glory filling it. Today, though, we are called to fully enter into His glory.

The first time, it might take you awhile to find the door to the holy place. But do not give up! The more often you go there, the more easily you will find it. When you enter, you will be blinded by its glory; the walls are covered with gold, it's so beautiful. The altar of incense is in that room. It is the place where your prayers go up to the Lord. He loves listening to you as you pour out your heart.

You might be tempted to stay in that room. However, while Heaven is open there, it is not Heaven itself. There is a huge, thick veil, and you can sense His glorious presence radiating through it. Only the high priest could go into the holy of holies once a year. Today—our Father longs for us to come in.

But it might not be that easy. You may look everywhere for the opening in the veil, struggling to find it, hungry to get into the presence of the Lord. Sometimes you might get tired and frustrated, but do not give up! It is so worth it! And again, every time you go in it gets easier; each time you will find the way more easily than the last!

On the Other Side

And then you are through. You are standing on the other side, the splendor is beyond anything you have ever imagined. You are in a glorious hall, its beauty blinding you. And yet, all the beauty fades and you do not even care because your Daddy is there—that's all that counts. In the distance you can see a glorious light from His throne, and you are filled with joy in anticipation. Like a little child, your face radiating, you start running toward your Father. As you get closer, you see His arms outstretched wide, and you run and jump onto His lap, and He takes you into His arms. You let go of everything; time ceases, space ceases, all words cease. His love and glory fill you, and all you do is simply rest in Him. From time to time He lowers His head to whisper things in your ear.

That is where we need to be; everyone can go there. Once you have been there, you do not want to be anywhere else. And He longs even more for us to be there with Him than we want to be there. It is the place to live our lives from.

Have you wondered what your destiny is? Your primary destiny is sitting on your Daddy's lap.

I found a new depth and dimension in my relationship with God in October 2001, and continued to spend many hours in intimate embrace with the Lover of my soul. I had found the most important key to be able to go to Mali, one of the darkest places in the earth, all alone, at the hand of my heavenly Father, with nothing but Him—intimacy.

Mentors

God continued the equipping process during my two years in Kansas City, taking it to a whole new level. I was on the ministry team at the International House of Prayer, enjoying the opportunity to pour out, and started serving at the Healing Rooms there during my second year, having an opportunity to practice the gift of healing.

In Jill Austin's classes, I loved the awesome encounters with God that we had, and Jill also gave us opportunities to be God's vessels. A few times a year she held a conference where we were her ministry team. They were great times of learning from a powerful carrier of God's glory. Jill had such a heart to produce spiritual children with a double-portion, and she poured out her life to us. I could see so much in her when I ministered, and the prophetic gifting in me increased dramatically. I remember times at her meetings when I was just amazed at the words coming out of my mouth, as I ministered through my spiritual mom's anointing.

I loved Jill very much, and I am honored to be one of her double-portion children she always wanted to have. Even after I left Kansas City, I tried to attend as many of her conferences as possible, knowing in advance that I would meet with God. I wanted to bless her, support her, and do anything I could for her, whatever she needed done. It was an honor to support her financially, even sacrificially, carrying her bag, making phone calls for her, or getting something she needed. The Lord deepened our relationship after I left for Mali. Unfortunately, occasions to get together were few as I was on the other side of the world. When I was ordained by Harvest International Ministry in the summer of 2008, I could have not been more blessed that she was there and prayed and prophesied over me. And I was deeply honored when she became one of the founding board members of *Healing 2 The Nations International* (the ministry I founded) after our incorporation in America in 2008.

I had found a spiritual mom, and was so blessed by this precious relationship. I loved her heart, loved how she looked for ways to prepare the way before me. I had many hopes and was looking forward to many more adventures with Jill. She was planning on coming to Mali for the first time for our fifth anniversary glory conference in November 2009. But then months before this conference, she suddenly and unexpectedly went to be with her Beloved. I believe she got one glimpse of the beauty of the Lover of her soul, and chose to remain with Him for all eternity. The Lord had given me a mom, and He had taken her away, just over a year after I had lost my spiritual dad.

To this day, I am praying for the Lord to give me new fathers and mothers in the spirit on this earth. We need them in the Body of Christ. Children can only flourish in their destiny if they have fathers and mothers cheering them on. Will you be a father? Will you be a mother?

We need divine enabling and encounters to be able to fulfill our destinies. We need to be equipped with the necessary tools to be able to fulfill our calling, and we need the corresponding spiritual gifts. We are all called to speak in tongues and should persevere until we have this precious gift from the Lord. But we need much more than that, whether it be gifts of healing or prophecy or any of the other gifts God bestows. Another helpful, though not essential, component of our enabling are spiritual parents who mentor us, as well as prophetic words that change things in the heavenly realm to prepare the way for us to walk into our destinies.

Finally, all the equipping and enabling is not worth anything if we have not found the intimate relationship with our Creator God that He wants us to have with Him and where all the gifts flow from as a by-product. Let's become intimate Lovers of God, and may that be our first and foremost identity in His Kingdom.

God's children need mentors—spiritual fathers and mothers—so we can reach our full potential as we strive to enter into our destinies. In the same way, prophetic input makes a huge difference in our lives. While it is not essential, it is a powerful tool the Lord uses to speak to us, confirm and direct us. Scripture tells us that, "the one who prophe-sies speaks to people for their strengthening, encouraging and comfort" (1 Cor. 14:3). All throughout the Bible we see that matters had to be es-tablished by two or three witnesses (see 2 Cor. 13:1, 1 Tim. 5:19, Heb. 10:28). Most of all, we need to hear God for ourselves. When He calls us, He speaks to us directly. We need to check everything we hear against His Word; if it contradicts God's revealed Word in the Bible, we know it is not God we have heard.

Second, we need to seek counsel from those in authority over us or trustworthy friends who know us well.

Third, a prophetic word through someone who does not know us or our situation is a powerful way to confirm calling and bring great encouragement to move forward in the direction He would have us go.

Countless Christians never step out and fulfill their destinies for various reasons. One of them might be the absence of confirmation through other people and prophetic words. Yes, I had no prophetic words when God called me to Africa, and still I kept going forward as there was no shadow of doubt what God had called me to. However, the prophetic words while I was in Canada and in the U.S. not only encouraged me and confirmed what was in my heart, they also revealed my heart and calling to the church and the invisible world.

Words have creative power—power to give life or to kill—and prophetic words can establish order in the invisible world and prepare the path for what God has spoken publicly. In July 2004, a year after I had gone to Mali, Jill Austin prophesied at a conference that I was an apostle. I had known that that calling was on me for many years, but had never said that to anyone because the fear of God was on me. I believe that Jill speaking it out prophetically positioned me in the invisible and visible world and made a difference in my work. (As a side note, I do not believe in titles. In my opinion, our lives speak loudly about our place in the Kingdom of God. If I have to actually *tell* someone I'm an apostle (or whatever else), then something is wrong. Let us simply love Jesus and serve Jesus without worrying about putting great-sounding titles on our business cards. I do not think that God is impressed. He is impressed with selfless lovers who will do whatever is on His heart.)

In November 2002, I experienced the life-changing power of a prophetic word when Kim Terrell and his friend prayed and prophesied over me. Not only was the power of God visibly on me, but God created in me a love for children as the words were spoken. And He also encouraged me that the hard times ahead were times of pruning me. That day I received a most important prophetic word when I was told that 2004 would be the year of great breakthrough.

Breakthrough

My first year in Mali was extremely hard. I was finally in my Promised Land, but it was still a far cry from seeing the vision He had given me fulfilled. I had no clue how to get there. I had to be patient—once again—and wait for God's timing. Yes, my neighbor came to know the Lord two months after my arrival. Yes, we started a weekly Bible study and time of worship. Yes, we did a little bit of evangelism. However, all I really did was teach German at the Malian high school and wait. It was a very lonely time, humanly speaking, while my Daddy in Heaven was the only One with me. I felt trapped in Mali since I had a commitment to the school.

Yet, throughout this difficult time, I held on to that word from 2002 that 2004 would be the year of breakthrough. I told God I would hold on through the end of the year, believing His promise. And of course, the breakthrough came just before the year ended. Jill did not only prophesy over me in July, but again in September, and I believe her words were heard in Heaven as well as on earth.

I returned to Mali rejuvenated, re-envisioned, and things started happening one after another. After a month of prayer and fasting, we had the first service of Centre Apostolique Malien on November 28, 2004. And then the Lord spoke to me to do two things—organize a Christmas Party for street children, and a healing service on New Year's Eve. We did both, and they were key for our moving forward. The breakthrough was completed, literally, on the last day, during the last hours even, of 2004.

I thank God for His word that helped me to hold on to Him until the hard time of waiting and difficulty was over! Was it necessary? No. I would probably have held on and continued in Mali anyway. However, God gave me a little gift that made it easier to keep going. We need those little gifts from our heavenly Father. He is so gracious and loves pouring out gifts over His children.

I love being prophesied over—of course testing the prophecy is necessary—and I love prophesying. I had longed for that gift and prayed for that gift for years, and the Lord heard my cry as He Himself tells us to, "eagerly desire gifts of the Spirit, especially prophecy" (1 Cor. 14:1). Do you desire spiritual gifts? Do you desire them enough to pay the price? We need to become humble and pure vessels full of love. It is not about the vessel, but about what flows out of it. Let us prophesy in love and never forget who is the One who gave the word—not us, but God.

Healing

I love being healed—physically, emotionally, spiritually—and I love to be a carrier of healing. Jesus told us to, "Heal the sick, raise the dead, cleanse those who have leprosy, drive out demons. Freely you have received; freely give" (Matt. 10:8). I desired gifts of healing for years, and again He heard my cry. I paid the price and allowed Him to make me into the vessel that He could pour healing oil out of. I love seeing broken hearts restored. I love seeing broken relationships with God re-established. I love seeing bodies line up with God's will and be healed. I have no greater joy than to see the Bride of Christ becoming whole, without spot or blemish, being made ready for the great wedding day with her amazing Bridegroom Jesus.

What an honor to be His instrument and serve His Bride! What an honor to go to the nations, to the farthest corners of the world, the darkest places that have not seen light, and bring God's light, glory, and power—advancing His Kingdom! I cannot imagine anything more worthwhile, more rewarding, and more fulfilling. That is why the ministry God has entrusted to me is called *Healing 2 The Nations International*. My call is to the nations—yes, Mali is my home base—but it goes far beyond the borders of Mali. I want to see people from every language, tribe, and nation in front of the throne of God, and I will do anything, go anywhere the Father sends me to do my part in fulfilling this task. God is handing out nations today. Who will say yes?

God is in the business of healing. He brings spiritual healing as people come out of the kingdom of darkness and become children of the light. He brings emotional healing as He forgives our sins and heals us from the pains of this fallen world. He brings physical healing as He restores our bodies to work the way He intended. We are not under

Adam's curse of sickness, death, and misery any more. The second Adam, Jesus, has broken that curse over our lives. We now live in His fullness, seated in heavenly places (see Eph. 2:6), reflecting Jesus as His ambassadors in a fallen world.

Prophetic Input

We need divine enabling and encounter to be able to fulfill our destinies. We need to be equipped with the necessary tools to be able to fulfill our calling, and we need the according spiritual gifts.

We are all called to speak in tongues and should persevere until we have this precious gift from the Lord. But we need much more than that, whether it be gifts of healing or prophecy or any of the other gifts God bestows.

Another helpful, though not essential, component of our enabling are spiritual parents who mentor us, as well as prophetic words that change things in the heavenly realm to prepare the way for us to walk into our destinies.

Finally, all the equipping and enabling is not worth anything if we have not found the intimate relationship with our Creator God that He wants us to have with Him and where all the gifts flow from as a by-product. Let's become intimate Lovers of God, and may that be our first and foremost identity in His Kingdom.

Can you hear God's challenge resounding through eternity? "Ask Me, and I will make the nations your inheritance, the ends of the earth your possession" (Ps. 2:8). Who has the courage to respond? Who will stand up and give to God what He longs to have? Who will fulfill the desire of God's heart? "Lift up your heads, you gates; be lifted up, you ancient doors, that the King of glory may come in" (Ps. 24:7).

Let us be forerunners who prepare the way for the coming of the King of glory in all His splendor! May He come through the gates of our cities and nations so they can fulfill their destinies and be ready for the great wedding feast of the lamb.

Maranatha, come Lord Jesus! (See Revelation 22:20.)

~

Lord, I love You, and I love being with You. Open my eyes to see You more, open my ears to hear You even more. Holy Spirit, take me by the hand and lead me into the throne room. Reveal the Father to me. Draw me into the arms of Jesus. I long for Your manifest presence in my life. I want to be ruined by Your love forever so that nothing but You matters. Lord, transform me, encounter me, wreck me forever with Your love and Your glory. May I never be content with anything less than You. Increase my hunger for You, and fill it with Your living waters. Thank You that everything else will flow out of our intimacy. Thank You that there is healing, provision, and equipping in Your presence. Thank You that I will walk in Your fullness, doing the works that Jesus did. Thank You that You have chosen me to be Your ambassador in this dark world. I say yes to You. Yes, I want to fulfill every task You have for me. I want to be one who dares to ask for a nation. I want to be one who prepares the way for the King of glory to come into cities and nations and see them transformed. Thank You for the privilege of presenting a nation to You the day of the great wedding feast!

Change Points

1. You need to have an intimate relationship with your God; and second, you need to be equipped with divine power to do the works that Jesus did. The second flows out of the first.

2. When God sets you free, not only will His love and tangible presence flow unhindered in your life, but the gifts of prophecy and healing will increase.

3. How much time do you spend speaking in tongues? Allow Him to edify you and refocus you as Holy Spirit prays through you.

4. Have you found the most important key—intimacy with Him?

5. You need to be equipped with the necessary tools to be able to fulfill your calling, and you need the corresponding spiritual gifts.

Contact the Author

Claudia would love to hear how you have been blessed and encouraged by this book. She is available to come to your church or group to minister, or to share about the work in Africa. Please contact her by email if you would like to invite her.

Healing 2 The Nations International is a not-for-profit organization registered in the USA. All proceeds from the sale of this book go directly to the ministry so the work in Africa can continue. Thank you for enabling her to rescue street children, feed the poor and widows, preach the Gospel and establish churches in an unreached nation.

For more information about Claudia, the ministry,
and all newsletters quoted in this book, write to:
Healing 2 The Nations Intl.
PO Box 76738
Colorado Springs, CO 80970

Or visit her Website:
www.healing2thenations.net

Email Claudia at:
claudia@healing2thenations.net

Additional copies of this book and other book titles from DESTINY IMAGE[TM] EUROPE are available at your local bookstore.

We are adding new titles every month!

To view our complete catalog online, visit us at:
www.eurodestinyimage.com

Send a request for a catalog to:

Via della Scafa 29/14
65013 Città Sant'Angelo (Pe) ITALY
Tel. +39 085 4716623 • +39 085 8670146
info@eurodestinyimage.com

"Changing the world, one book at a time."

Are you an author?

Do you have a "today" God-given message?

CONTACT US

We will be happy to review your manuscript for the possibility of publication:

publisher@eurodestinyimage.com
http://www.eurodestinyimage.com/pages/AuthorsAppForm.htm